THE UNKNOWN NERUDA

Pablo Neruda
THE UNKNOWN NERUDA
❦

Poems selected, translated & introduced by
Adam Feinstein

PUBLICATIONS
2019

Published by Arc Publications,
Nanholme Mill, Shaw Wood Road
Todmorden OL14 6DA, UK
www.arcpublications.co.uk

978 1911469 13 1 (pbk)
978 1911469 14 8 (hbk)

ACKNOWLEDGEMENTS
The author extends his heartfelt gratitude to all those with
whom he has enjoyed so many fascinating conversations about
Pablo Neruda's life and work. His special thanks go to Hernán
Loyola, Jason Wilson and Dominic Moran for their illuminating
insights, and to his family and many other friends.

Design by Tony Ward
Printed in Great Britain by T.J. International Ltd,
Padstow, Cornwall

Cover picture:
Angelo Cozzi / Mondadori via Getty Images

Supported using public funding by
ARTS COUNCIL
ENGLAND
LOTTERY FUNDED

'Arc Publications Classics: New Translations
of Great Poets of the Past'
Series Editor: Jean Boase-Beier

To my loving mother, Elaine,
who has taught me so much of what I know
about poetry, translation —
and life itself.

CONTENTS

Introduction / 9

I have been translating the work of Pablo Neruda for two decades or more, but there is a particular thrill in knowing that the vast majority of the poems in this collection have never been translated into English before. This is extremely rare for a Nobel Prize-winning poet – one who was called 'the greatest poet of the twentieth century in any language' by Gabriel García Márquez and 'the King Midas of poetry' by Carlos Fuentes. These poems also took me, as a fellow-traveller, translator and biographer, along an exciting path: Neruda's voyage of self-discovery (and so many of his poems are about journeys, in one sense of another). That voyage took him from his lonely childhood in Temuco, southern Chile, absorbing multiple literary influences, via the mature Neruda, with his assured voice (or voices) and worldwide fame, to the tragic last few months of his life in Santiago, sick and aware of both his own impending death and the death of the Chile he knew and loved. And even beyond the grave, to some of the poems he intended to leave the world for his seventieth birthday, in 1974. My hope is that this collection will also sweep you, the reader, on this same exhilarating journey.

Translating Neruda is a challenge. The tightrope walk between meaning and music is particularly perilous in his case. One of Neruda's contemporary translators, William O'Daly, has stated: 'I know of no greater or more natural musician, in the canon of Spanish-language poetry, than Neruda. His own voice and the ways in which he articulates his poems, the patterns of sound, integrate beautifully with the softnesses and natural movements of the Spanish language.'[1] The Spanish poet, Gabriel Celaya, showed one of his poems to both Neruda and to Neruda's great friend, Federico García Lorca, in Madrid in 1935. Lorca made some brief comments about the structure of Celaya's poem, whereas Neruda went through each line of the poem meticulously

---

[1] See interview with William O'Daly in *Translation Review* (University of Texas, No. 67, 2004), p. 6

and, according to Celaya, 'in total contrast to Lorca, showed himself to be, as in his own poetry, more concerned with the minimal units of the poem, the right adjectives, no wasted images, functional sounds, than with the form and overall structure of the poem. The accumulation of correct words or lovely details takes precedence for him, like a primitive, over the general concept.'[2]

Like virtually any act of human collaboration, translation requires communication between translator and reader. It is also, of course, a dialogue between the translator and the source-language writer. Walter Benjamin spoke of the concept of 'double indebtedness': the original requires translation and is, therefore, indebted to the translation, just as the translation requires the original and is, therefore, indebted to the original. George Steiner, in his classic work, *After Babel*, describes translation as 'hermeneutic motion', whereby a translator 'invades, extracts and brings home.'[3]

Neruda has sold more books than any other twentieth-century Spanish-language poet, and he is probably the most translated modern poet in the world. He published more than forty collections of poems. This has led some critics, absurdly in my view, to condemn the 'unevenness' of his output. His younger compatriot, Nicanor Parra, brilliantly defended Neruda against this charge, pointing out: 'The Andes are also uneven.' Neruda sought to re-invent himself in each book – and the translator also needs new tools, or at least a new approach, as he tackles each fresh challenge.

Pablo Neruda was born Ricardo Eliecer Neftalí Reyes Basoalto on 12 July 1904 in Parral, in the central wine-producing region of Chile. His real mother, Rosa Neftalí Basoalto Opazo, a primary school teacher, died of tuberculosis on 14 September that year, less than two months after giving birth to him. Neruda did not of course, remember her directly, but only through a photograph which he said showed a woman dressed in black, slender and thoughtful. I

[2] Gabriel Celaya: 'El poeta del Tercer Día de la Creación,' *Revista de Occidente* (Madrid, No. 36, 1972)
[3] George Steiner: *After Babel: Aspects of Language and Translation* (Oxford: Oxford University Press, 1998), p. 314

have selected an extremely touching poem dedicated to his mother, 'Luna' (Moon) written in 1922. Notice the association of the moon with a negative idea – his mother's death. The moon would often have negative connotations in Neruda's later poems, too, especially in his great work, *Residencia en la tierra* (Residence on Earth).

At the age of two, the young boy, together with his train driver father, José del Carmen, and his stepmother, Trinidad Candia Marverde (the 'Mamadre' whom Neftalí adored and 'whose gentle shadow watched over my childhood')[4], moved to Temuco. It was a town without a past, a town made of wood. Neruda would never forget the smell of that timber and the sound of rain falling on the zinc roofs. At the time, the town was, as the great Neruda scholar, Hernán Loyola, has put it, 'the centre of the Chilean Far West and, therefore, of the febrile social and economic activity in which young Neftalí's childhood developed'.[5] For the young boy, who was timid and sickly, literary activity quickly became his passion – both reading and writing.

His major poetic influences, as a voracious adolescent reader, were the great Nicaraguan 'modernista' poet,' Rubén Darío (from whom the young Neftalí borrowed imagery, as well as persistent use of rhyme and the alexandrine), and the French Romantics and symbolists (especially Baudelaire, Rimbaud and Verlaine). Neruda's passion for Baudelaire, in particular, was life-long. The Mexican writer, Carlos Fuentes, confirmed to me that when, as Chilean Ambassador in Paris in the early 1970s, Neruda held a meeting with President Georges Pompidou to discuss Chile's foreign debt, the two men spent the entire two hours discussing Baudelaire's poetry instead.[6] Walt Whitman was another key influence. (Many years later, Neruda's carpenter, Rafita, was doing some work around the poet's Pacific Coast house at Isla Negra when he spotted the portrait of a bearded

---

[4] See Pablo Neruda: *Memoirs* (London: Souvenir Press, 1977), p. 20
[5] Hernán Loyola: *Neruda: La biografía literaria* (Santiago: Editorial Planeta Chilena, 2006), p. 52
[6] Adam Feinstein: *Pablo Neruda: A Passion for Life* (London: Bloomsbury, 2013), p. 385

man on the wall. 'Is that your grandfather?' Rafita asked. 'Yes,' Neruda replied. In fact, it was a portrait of Whitman.) Susan Sontag wrote that Whitman 'tried to see beyond the difference between beauty and ugliness' and also that he 'saw no contradiction between making art an instrument of identification with the community and aggrandising the artist as a heroic, romantic, self-expressing ego.'[7] Neruda, too, was an aesthetic democrat, and frequently emulated Whitman's euphoric humanism – but he also saw the poet as an important figure. Indeed, after a visit to Brazil in 1945, Neruda would declare: 'A poet who reads his poems to 130,000 people is not the same man and cannot keep writing in the same way.'[8]

Neftali had access to many books in the library of the old poet, Augusto Winter, in Puerto Saavedra, the beach resort where the family would go in the summer holidays. And when Neruda decided to show his early poems to the head teacher of the girls' school in Temuco in 1920, she not only recommended that he read Tolstoy, Dostoyevsky, Chekhov and Gorky and the Scandinavians, Hamsun and Lagerlöf, but she lent him the books. That head teacher's name was Lucila Godoy – but under her pseudonym, Gabriela Mistral, she would go on to win the Nobel Prize for Literature in 1945, the first Latin American to do so. According to Loyola, 'for the provincial Neftalí, the geography of culture is global'.[9]

The first text Neruda ever published was actually a piece of prose, entitled 'Entusiasmo y perseverancia' (Enthusiasm and Perseverance), in the Temuco daily, La Mañana, in 1917, just after his thirteenth birthday. Soon, he was writing poems. The first known one, apart from a postcard he dedicated to his stepmother in 1915, was 'Nocturno' (Nocturne), dated 18 April 1918. However, his father did not consider poetry a manly profession, and when he became wise to the fact that his son was furtively publishing his early poems in the Santiago magazine, Corre-Vuela, José del Carmen burst

[7] See Susan Sontag: On Photography (New York: Penguin Books, 1979), pp. 27 & 30
[8] Pablo Neruda: Memoirs, p. 313
[9] Loyola, op. cit., p. 97

into Neftalí's bedroom in a fury, tossing all his notebooks out of the window on to the patio below. Many years later, on receiving the Nobel Prize for Literature in 1971, Neruda recalled: 'I was the most abandoned of poets, and my poetry was regional, painful and drenched in rain.' But, in one of the great paradoxes of twentieth-century culture, his severe, bearded father would unwittingly fuel the young boy's poetic imagination by driving him through the startlingly beautiful forests of southern Chile on his locomotive. Neruda would go on to become, in Dominic Moran's words, 'one of the greatest nature poets in the Spanish language'.[10]

The first few poems in this collection come from three notebooks written by hand by the young Neftalí containing a total of nearly 190 original poems. On the death of his beloved half-sister, Laura, in 1977, these three notebooks (together with Neruda's entire library) were entrusted to a presumed nephew of hers, Rafael Aguayo Quezada, a professor at the Universidad Católica in Temuco. They were put up for auction at Sotheby's in London in 1982 and published in their entirety by Hernán Loyola in Volume 4 of his superb edition of Neruda's complete works as *Los cuadernos de Neftalí Reyes* (The Neftalí Reyes Notebooks).

Neruda's mood when writing many of these early poems was buffeted in a precarious pendulum of depression alternating with euphoria. As early as 1918, Neruda's poetry features Darío-like melancholy. 'Lo estéril' (Sterility, p. 39), the first poem I have selected for this edition, written in November 1919, is drenched in a pessimistic sense of defeat. The lovely 'En la ventana' (At the Window, p. 39), written in February 1920, begins gloomily but ends with defiant passion for life. The delightful 'No seas como el árbol primifloro' (The First Flowers, p. 41), also written in 1920, is probably the very first poem which he signed under his new pseudonym of Pablo Neruda. This is interesting, because it is generally believed that he changed his name (and then fled to Santiago in 1921) to escape his father's clutches. But he was still living in Temuco at this point.

The origins of the pen name remain shrouded in mystery.

---

[10] Dominic Moran: *Pablo Neruda* (London: Reaktion Books, 2009), p. 17

13

He usually claimed in interviews that he could not remember where the name Pablo Neruda came from. This seems scarcely credible. Interviewed by the Uruguayan magazine, *Marcha*, in 1971, he insisted, instead, that he had come across a short story signed by the Czech writer, Jan Neruda. But there are many other intriguing hypotheses. As a life-long devotee of detective stories, could he have been inspired by a character named Norman Neruda in Arthur Conan Doyle's first Sherlock Holmes novel, *A Study in Scarlet*? Might the young Neftalí have seen a poster sporting the names of two violinists – Pablo de Sarasate and Wilhelmine Maria Franziska Neruda – as the Germany-based Chilean doctor, Enrique Robertson, proposes?[11] Jason Wilson sees a literary debt to the French Romantic, Gérard de Nerval (the similarities in their surnames having first been pointed out by the Spanish poet, Juan Larrea, in 1967).[12] As for the 'Pablo', the Uruguayan critic, Emir Rodríguez Monegal, suggested that the Pablo was Neruda's homage to Paul Verlaine (surprisingly, Verlaine's first published poem was signed as 'Pablo Verlaine'). Might the Pablo come from Dante's Paolo (we know Neruda was reading Dante from early on in his life)? Whatever the origins, the name Pablo Neruda appeared in print for the very first time in the Chilean students' union journal, *Claridad*, on 22 January 1921 (in a laudatory note by Fernando Ossorio – itself a pseudonym for the Chilean critic, Raúl Silva Castro), accompanied by six of Neruda's poems.

At around this time, Neruda's poetry begins to reveal a new optimism (though still in taut dialogue with an instinctive impulse towards existential anguish). The remarkable 'Primavera' (A New Spring, p. 43), written in September 1920, contains elements of both states of mind. Significantly, we see a similar dialogue in many of Rubén Darío's poems.

We translators and critics must constantly be wary of over-interpretation, however seductive this may be. The Chilean psychologist, Luis Rubilar Solís, has gone to the extreme of assuring us that every time Neruda refers to a rose in a poem, he is actually recalling the mother (Rosa)

---

[11] See Enrique Robertson: 'Pablo Neruda, el enigma inaugural', http://webs.ucm.es/info/especulo/numero22/neruda.html
[12] See Jason Wilson: *A Companion to Pablo Neruda: Evaluating Neruda's Poetry* (London: Tamesis, 2008), p. 15

he never knew. Neruda himself would have mocked this suggestion. But then he rejected all attempts to explain the meanings of symbols in his poems. He told the Argentinian journalist, Rita Guibert, in 1970: 'The sea, fish, birds exist for me in a material sense... When I see a dove, I call it a dove. Whether or not it is present at that moment, for me it has a form, which may be subjective or objective, but it is still a dove.'

Whether or not we take this statement at face value, it should, at the very least, encourage caution. Readers will notice that some of the early poems written in Temuco selected for this edition contain religious imagery. Do not be deceived. Neruda was never inspired by religious feeling – I believe that when he does introduce religious imagery or symbolism into these early poems, he did so partly in homage to other poets he admired at the time, including Rubén Darío, or as an act of reverence and love for his stepmother, Trinidad. She was indeed a church-goer and took young Neftalí to a service on one occasion. Although he could not share her fervour, he clearly respected it. But the metaphysics in some of these early poems is not mystical. As Jason Wilson has usefully pointed out, for Neruda, as it was for the Spanish Golden Age poet, Francisco de Quevedo (who would become a huge influence), metaphysics is immensely physical.[13]

Wilson has detected other evident literary debts: the restlessness of Rimbaud (whose poetry Neruda knew by heart when he could often not remember his own), Mallarmé (especially the sense of *ennui* in the opening line of Mallarmé's famous 'Brise marine': 'La chair est triste, hélas! Et j'ai lu tous les livres – The flesh is sad, alas, And I've read all the books') and the emotional intensity of the Spanish Romantic poet, Gustavo Adolfo Bécquer.[14]

In March 1921, Neruda left Temuco for the Chilean capital, Santiago, which he recalled in his *Memoirs* as smelling 'of gas fumes and coffee.'[15] His purported aim was to study to

---

[13] Wilson, *op. cit.*, p. 11
[14] *Idem*, pp. 36-37
[15] *Ibid*.

be a French teacher. But just as important was to establish a safe distance from his father so he could continue to write in freedom. Soon after his arrival in Santiago, the young student was enjoying a new bohemian existence, with friendships and love affairs which represented a dramatic contrast with his lonely, sickly childhood in Temuco. This was also the moment when the literary avant-garde was triumphing worldwide. For 1922 was the year that James Joyce published *Ulysses*, T. S. Eliot brought out *The Waste Land* and, closer to home, the great Peruvian poet, César Vallejo, published *Trilce* and, in Argentina, Oliverio Girondo brought out *Veinte poemas para ser leídos en el tranvía* (Twenty Poems to be Read on the Tram).

Neruda began to write articles in the student journal, *Claridad* (including some revealing a very early concern for the socially under-privileged and downtrodden). And if we are to believe his own account, between 1921 and 1923, he also started writing poetry feverishly (at the rate of up to five poems a day). *Claridad* published a number of these poems – among them (in November 1922) the striking 'Palabras de amor' (Words of Love, p. 45), which I have selected for this edition. This could almost be an early draft of one of the celebrated *Veinte poemas de amor y una canción desesperada* (Twenty Love Poems and a Song of Despair) published two years later. Notice the reference to a starry night (a precursor of Poem 20); the sense of elusiveness of the woman (and yet paradoxically, also, the feeling that she 'knows everything' about him, a theme to which Neruda will also return in the *Twenty Love Poems)*; and the sense of words as objects to be gathered (like the necklace of words in Poem 5 of the 1924 collection).

For Hernán Loyola, Neruda's poetry of this period reveals evident influences of the emerging 'codes' of the new modernity. But in these early years of the 1920s, his poems continued to hover in what Loyola has called a 'precarious equilibrium' between the passion of idealistic optimism and a growing sense of personal failure, of defeat. Many of these early poems are indeed laced with feelings of exclusion, weakness and impotence – and sometimes an obsession with death. This obsession was not whimsical: many of his friends died of tuberculosis at this time. Indeed, at around the moment his first book, *Crepusculario* was published in Santiago in 1923, one of his most important lovers in Santiago, Albertina Azócar, was undergoing an emergency operation for peritonitis, which was usually fatal in the first few decades of the twentieth century.

Crepusculario is a typical Nerudian neologism, meaning something like 'Collection of Twilights.' Jason Wilson argues that the most likely inspiration for the title was Baudelaire's prose poem, 'Le Crépuscule du soir' (Evening Twilight), although he also suggests an oblique homage to the Argentinian 'modernista' poet, Leopoldo Lugones, who had published two books calls *Crepúsculos del jardín* and *Lunario sentimental* in 1905 and 1909, respectively. We know that Neruda considered Lugones' poetry to be 'rich in gifts', because he later said as much in a letter to his Argentinian epistolary friend, Héctor Eandi, from the Far East.[16]

To pay for the publication of *Crepusculario*, Neruda pawned the watch his father had given him, as well as his black suit. But most authors will recognise the thrill of seeing that first book appear in print, a thrill Neruda described magnificently in his memoirs, *Confieso que he vivido* (I Confess That I've Lived): 'That moment when the first book appears, with its ink fresh and its paper still crisp, that enchanted and ecstatic moment, with the sounds of wings beating or the first flower opening on the conquered height, that moment comes only once in the poet's lifetime.'[17]

The poems in *Crepusculario* were written between May 1920 and May 1923. Some were new versions of poems he had 'tried out' in the *Notebooks of Neftalí Reyes*. There are intense outbursts of crisis, of romantic exaltation, in which Neruda refuses to concede defeat.

At times, a second, intimate personal voice tempers the expansive romanticism. In fact, Neruda's poetry would always be marked by these two poles – and in his 1950 epic book, *Canto general*, they combine in one and the same work. (In that later work – a book about public and private betrayals – he not only condemned the brutality of the

---

[16] See Wilson, *op. cit.*, p. 27
[17] *Memoirs*, p. 51

Spanish Conquistadors four hundred years earlier on the American continent, but the personal, present-day treachery of his own President, Gabriel González Videla, for turning against the Communists – including Neruda – who had helped him bring him to power.)

Jason Wilson maintains that part of the mood of *Crepusculario* is characterised by Neruda's 'disgust with his new urban surroundings where love has been commercialised into sex and his natural self contaminated by industrial and city artifice'.[18] There is some truth in this – and it was a feeling which would invade him again in the early 1930s when he was posted to Buenos Aires as Chilean consul. Nevertheless, I am convinced that Neruda was as profoundly relieved to have found in Santiago a wide circle of friends and lovers as he was to return to bohemian gregariousness in Argentina after six years of desolate isolation in the Orient.

The sense of alienation from city life undoubtedly pervades one of the poems I have selected from *Crepusculario*, 'Barrio sin luz' (Suburban Gloom, p. 59), with its reference to the

City of soot and vengeance,
the grim, grey filth of the suburbs,
workers hunched in offices,
under their bosses' turbid glare.

The other poems I have chosen from this first book include the lovely 'Morena, la besadora' (Kiss Me, My Dark-Skinned One, p. 49), which, as Wilson correctly notes, ends, like Rubén Dario's erotic poem 'Ite, missa est', as a blasphemy, 'Amén' (the rest of Neruda's poem has been naming parts of a woman's body).[19] I have also selected one of the most famous poems in *Crepusculario*, 'Farewell' (Farewell, p. 51). *Crepusculario* itself remains relatively little-known – hence the inclusion of a number of its poems in this collection. The theme of 'Farewell' is the joy of departure and freedom from commitment (and also, according to Wilson, a secret homage to Rimbaud's prose poem, 'Adieu', from his 1873 collection, *Une Saison en enfer*).[20] And finally, 'Padre' (Father,

---

[18] Wilson, *op. cit.*, p. 41
[19] *Idem*, p. 35
[20] *Idem*, p. 43

18

p. 57) – with its surprisingly tender allusion to 'your gentle eyes', given the chilly relations between Neruda and José del Carmen at the time.

On one of his visits back to Temuco, during the Chilean summer holidays in January 1923, Neruda decided to take a last look out at the stunning night sky before going to sleep. He later recalled that he suddenly dashed to his desk and wrote, with a thumping heart, the first poem of what would end up as a book called *El hondero entusiasta* (The Ardent Slingsman). This book had a chequered history – at least, it did according to Neruda's account. He claimed he showed that first poem to a friend, Aliro Oyarzún, who immediately suggested that it bore the influence of the Uruguayan poet, Carlos Sabat Ercasty. Purportedly in shock, Neruda sent the poem to Sabat Ercasty himself, who replied: 'I have rarely read such a magnificently successful poem, but I have to tell you: there are echoes of Sabat Ercasty in your verse.' Neruda's response, according to his memoirs, was to hide *El hondero entusiasta* away in a drawer and not publish it for another decade. In fact, as Dominic Moran has pointed out, Neruda already knew Sabat Ercasty's poetry well and had been corresponding with the Uruguayan *before* sending him that initial poem.[21]

Influence or imitation? The line is particularly blurred when you are still a young poet and reading voraciously. The extract from *El hondero entusiasta* I have selected for this edition shows the traces of Surrealist 'inspiration' or, as Jason Wilson notes, of dictation as defined by André Breton as 'thought in the absence of any control exercised by reason, beyond all aesthetic or moral preoccupations'.[22] Many of the images in this extract – the bow and arrow, the night of stars, and above all the unattainable woman – would be carried over into the *Veinte poemas de amor*. It is clear, in fact, that *El hondero entusiasta* was the book Neruda had intended to publish directly after *Crepusculario* and before the *Twenty Love Poems*.

---

[21] Moran, *op. cit.*, p. 31
[22] Wilson, *op. cit.*, p. 78

The *Veinte poemas de amor,* published by Nascimento in 1924, would make Neruda's name. By 1961, they had sold a million copies worldwide and by 2004, the centenary of his birth, seven million. Yet, as Dominic Moran rightly reminds us, on the book's initial publication, it was greeted 'with a mixture of nervous bemusement and chilly sarcasm.'[23]

Tentativa de hombre infinito (Endeavour of the Infinite Man), from which I have selected just a single short extract, was one of three books Neruda published in 1926 – all brought out by his remarkable Azores-born publisher, Carlos George Nascimento, who took a risk on so many writers just starting out on their own literary careers. The two other books by Neruda published by Nascimiento in 1926 were his only novella, *El habitante y su esperanza* (The Inhabitant and his Hope) and *Anillos* (Rings), a book of prose poems co-written with his friend, Tomás Lago. *Tentativa* is Neruda's early avant-garde experiment – and one of which he always claimed to be proud. It is in fifteen sections, none of which contain any punctuation whatsoever (in later years, he would joke about the possibility of another literary endeavour: namely, a collection of poems consisting only of punctuation!).

Jaime Alazraki insisted that *Tentativa* was the first collection of 'surrealist making written in the Spanish language.'[24] Jason Wilson sees the poem as a Rimbaud-like 'journey, beyond rationality, into the dark, endless self,' but adds that 'the form of the poem moves from Rimbaud to his disciples, Apollinaire and Mallarmé.'[25] And Wilson also claims that there are 'countless' echoes of Neruda's compatriot, Vicente Huidobro. Before the two men fell out (for both aesthetic and personal reasons), Neruda admired the Huidobro of the *Poemas árticos,* a series of short poems published in Spain in 1918, also totally lacking in punctuation and notable for free-floating lines.[26]

From Chile's Far West (Temuco), via Santiago, Neruda

[23] Pablo Neruda: *Veinte poemas de amor y una canción desesperada,* ed. Dominic Moran (Manchester: Manchester University Press, 2007), p. ix
[24] Jaime Alazraki: *Poética y poesía de Pablo Neruda.* (New York: Las Américas, 1965), pp. 42-43
[25] Wilson, *op. cit.,* p. 81
[26] *Ibid.*

moved to the Far East. Tired of what had become the empty bohemianism of life in the Chilean capital, he sought and was offered his first diplomatic posting – as Chilean consul in the Burmese capital, Rangoon, of all places – in 1927. Neruda filled the desolate six years of alienation in the Orient with one immensely important and passionate love affair (with a native Burmese woman known only, to us at least, as Josie Bliss), and with avid reading, particularly Marcel Proust (from whom he learned to travel within his own mind 'to relive my own life, to recover the hidden feelings I had almost lost within myself in my long absence', as he put it in his *Memoirs*[27]) and D. H. Lawrence. Dominic Moran has brilliantly elucidated the vast influence Lawrence had on a number of the key poems in Neruda's great 1933 collection, *Residencia en la tierra* (Residence on Earth).

In 1930, Neruda married for the first time, in Batavia (modern-day Jakarta). His bride was the Anglo-Indonesian María Antonia Hagenaar (whom he called Maruca). He would later admit that he had married out of loneliness and, from the very start, it was not a happy union. The extraordinary 'Oda tórrida' (Torrid Ode, p. 65) is not remotely like any of the enchanting odes Neruda would write to ordinary objects (a tomato, an onion, even to his socks) from 1954 onwards, making the ordinary extraordinary. He wrote this poem, with its overwhelming landslide of images, in Java in 1931, and some of his marital dissatisfaction is already emerging very clearly. The poem appeared in print only in June 1935, in a short-lived Chilean magazine called *Revista del Pacífico*. Edmundo Olivares has pointed out that its oppressive tone resembles that of poems like 'El joven monarca' (The Young Monarch) from *Residencia en la tierra*.[28] But as I have noted elsewhere, it also has an epic quality foreshadowing one of Neruda's greatest works, *Alturas de Macchu Picchu* (Heights of Machu Picchu).[29] And it may have been this epic feel which

[27] *Memoirs*, p. 98
[28] Edmundo Olivares Briones: *Pablo Neruda: Los caminos de Oriente. Tras las huellas del poeta itinerante, 1927-1933.* (Santiago: LOM Ediciones, 2000), p. 119
[29] See Feinstein: *Pablo Neruda, op. cit.,* p. 87

prompted Neruda not to include the poem in *Residence on Earth*. What is interesting is that he chose to read it at a recital to a packed audience in Santiago in May 1932, just a month after his return from the Orient with Maruca. There may be an element of public catharsis here.

If so, then this cathartic process continued in the peculiar 'Número y nombre' (Number and Name, p. 67), first published in the Chilean newspaper, *El Mercurio*, in November 1933. Neruda and Maruca had returned from the Orient to Chile in 1932 and they were now living in Buenos Aires, where Neruda was fulfilling his new consular position. As Loyola has noted, dreams (especially those of others) were a persistent motif in Neruda's poetry of this period. Other examples are the dream sequence in *El habitante y su esperanza*, 'Caballo de los sueños' (Horse of Dreams), which he wrote in 1927 and which would then be published in *Residencia en la tierra*, and 'Colección nocturna' (Night Collection) also from *Residence on Earth*.[30] Unusually, 'Número y nombre' is written entirely in heptasyllables. Neruda appears to be attempting to escape from his depression (provoked by his awareness of having married unwisely) and also his precarious economic situation. But Wilson has also argued that Neruda's exploration of dreams is surrealist because of its links with the previously mentioned French Romantic poet, Gérard de Nerval.[31]

'Severidad' (Severity, p. 71), a blistering attack on Neruda's critics and enemies, was written in Buenos Aires at the beginning of 1934. This was a fascinating and complex period of his life. He met Federico García Lorca in the Argentinian capital for the first time (Lorca was there for the première of his play *Bodas de Sangre* – Blood Wedding), and apart from his marital woes, he did not especially enjoy his diplomatic duties (although he fulfilled them gamely). It was at this time that he wrote his famous poem, 'Walking Around', in part describing this alienation from bureaucracy, although as Dominic Moran has valuably shown, it also bears the

---

[30] See Pablo Neruda: *Obras completas*, ed. Hernán Loyola (Barcelona: Galaxia Gutenberg, Círculo de Lectores, Vol. 4, 2001), p. 1244
[31] Wilson, *op. cit.*, p. 85

influence of both Lorca and D. H. Lawrence.[32]

Biographers like myself need to beware the perils of tying chronology too closely to a particular work of art. The temptations are potent – especially with a subject like Neruda, whose life and work are often so intimately interwoven. Just as 'Walking Around', for all its comic surrealism, has been described as one of the most pessimistic poems in the Spanish language when Neruda was enjoying a renewed social life after his Asian desolation, so the bitterness of 'Severidad' does not exactly chime with his current state of mind, either. In fact, the poem is even more acidic than other such assaults on his foes, such as 'No me rindo' (I'm Not Giving Up) in his 1964 collection, *Memorial de Isla Negra*. Loyola believes that it was Lorca himself who encouraged Neruda to respond to his literary critics. Neruda was, by nature, a timid man – which Lorca certainly was not – and the Spaniard appears to have incited the Chilean to reply energetically and aggressively to his foes in verse.[33] Indeed, it is no coincidence that 'Severidad' forms part of the little booklet, *Paloma por dentro* (A Dove Within) that Neruda and Lorca produced together in Buenos Aires in 1934 for their Argentinian friend, Sara Tornú, (Neruda wrote the poems and Lorca illustrated them with his decidedly macabre pencil drawings.)

Neruda's subsequent diplomatic posting – to Spain in 1934 – proved decisive. The Spanish Civil War, and especially Lorca's brutal murder by the fascists in August 1936, brought about what the Spanish critic, Amado Alonso, called Neruda's poetic 'conversion' – a dramatic metamorphosis from the anguished, inward-looking, poetry of his early books to poetry as a social and political weapon. Dominic Moran correctly points out that the re-encounter with the Spanish Golden Age poet, Francisco de Quevedo, in the mid-1930s, also cured Neruda of his obsession with death. Quevedo's influence, coupled with his own experiences in Spain, impelled Neruda to view death as 'a constitutive part of

---

[32] See *Cantalao*, Vol. 1 No. 1, 2013, pp. 26-35
[33] See Pablo Neruda: *Obras completas, op.cit.*, Vol. 4, p. 1246

a life that was greater than the sum of perishable, finite parts.'[34]

Neruda was not yet a Communist – although his new lover (and future second wife), the Argentinian painter, Delia del Carril, twenty years his senior, certainly was. She was also absent-minded (capable of serving soup with matchsticks floating in it), hugely talented and supremely cultured – and she was the only literary critic that he ever trusted. Not that, even here, he always took her advice: both Delia and his Soviet writer friend, Ilya Ehrenburg, warned him against over-using the word 'raíces' (roots). That did not stop him – and in fact, after Neruda returned to his Chilean roots by leaving Delia for Matilde Urrutia (the only Chilean of his three wives) in the mid-1950s, Neruda's use of 'raíces' accelerated.

If he was not yet formally committed to the Communist cause in the 1930s, he showed with a remarkable life-saving mission (which he later described as his favourite 'poem'), that he was capable of humanitarian actions, as well as words. In August 1939, he chartered a small fishing boat, the *Winnipeg*, and in it he dispatched more than 2,300 refugees from Franco's fascism (who had crossed the Pyrenees and were living in appalling conditions in French concentration camps) from Bordeaux in southern France to Valparaíso in Chile, where they arrived on 1 September 1939 – the day the Second World War broke out back in Europe. I was fortunate enough to interview some of the *Winnipeg* passengers whose lives Neruda saved. They included a number of children who would go on to play major roles in Chile's cultural and economic life: the painters Roser Bru and José Balmes, as well as the engineer and businessman Víctor Pey.

Neruda formally joined the Chilean Communist Party in 1945. As I have argued elsewhere[35], from that moment on, the absence of a loved one or an object would never be as sweet as her (or its) presence. Materialism (dialectic or otherwise) took hold of his poetry for good. But his was generally an emotional and aesthetic materialism, a sensory, telluric connection with the real world, which produced

---

[34] See Moran, *op. cit.*, p. 80
[35] See Feinstein: *Pablo Neruda: A Passion for Life*

24

some of the richest poetry in the Spanish language. And it inspired a humanism which he described five years later in his poem, 'A mi Partido' (To My Party), in *Canto general*, a short manifesto of love for fellow man, rather than political dogmatism or expediency.

Having said which, it has to be conceded that his 1954 collection, *Las uvas y el viento* (The Grapes and the Wind), published by Nascimento, is largely tainted by the kind of Socialist realism of which Andrei Zhdanov, the chief proponent of the concept back in 1934, would have been proud. I have, however, rescued nine very beautiful poems from this book which are unsoiled by political orthodoxy. And never again would Neruda fall into the trap of following any dogmatic party line as a poet – even if he remained loyal in his public declarations to the official Kremlin position for longer than many others would have liked. In any case, Neruda himself always denied he was a political poet and insisted that love was the central theme of his work. And the fact is that those who try and draw a perfectly formed dividing line between his political poems and his love poetry are misguided. Some of his most powerful love poems are also political, while some of his most intensely felt political poems are poems of passion (to a person or to a country).

It must also be remembered that most of the poems in *Las uvas y el viento* were written during the three years Neruda spent in exile – mostly in Europe. In 1948, he had stood up in the Chilean Senate and condemned his own President, Gabriel González Videla, for turning against the Communists who had helped him win power. After that act of courage, his senatorial immunity was lifted and he was forced underground for what he called 'a year of blind rats;' in hiding from the authorities. It is a year playfully depicted in Pablo Larraín's 2016 movie, *Neruda*, on which I was an adviser. (Among those who harboured Neruda during that year in hiding was the same Víctor Pey, whose life he had saved on the *Winnipeg* ten years earlier.) In February 1949, in another remarkable turn worthy of Hollywood, Neruda escaped across the Andes on horseback into Argentina and, from there, found his way to Europe using the passport of his Guatemalan friend, the future Nobel Prize-winning novelist Miguel Ángel Asturias.

Neruda described the eventful three years in exile in Europe (from 1949 to 1952) in his gloriously life-affirming (though not always entirely reliable) memoirs. Several of the poems from *Las uvas y el viento* which I have selected for the present edition also portray this extraordinary time of his life. He depicts his intense friendship with Pablo Picasso in the remarkably dense poem 'Llegada a Puerto Picasso' (Arriving at Port Picasso, p. 117) – in some ways, an attempt to recreate elements of the painting *Guernica* in verse. 'La policía' (The Police, p. 89) captures both Neruda's irritation and his mischievous sense of fun at the constant presence of the police. (At one point, he was even chased down a Venice canal on a gondola by the *carabinieri* after he refused to refrain from making political declarations during his stay in Italy.) 'La policía' reminds me in tone, strangely enough, of the Czech poet (and scientist), Miroslav Holub, who also couched serious concerns in conversational registers. Of the other Italian friends mentioned in these poems, Renato Guttuso was the prominent painter, while the umbrella brandished by Alberto Moravia's wife, Elsa Morante, is a reference to the wonderful moment when she used it as a weapon to prod a policeman at Naples railway station and, in so doing, persuaded the authorities to allow Neruda to remain on Italian soil.

In those three years in European exile in the early-1950s, Neruda juggled his life between his second wife, Delia (whom he had married in Mexico in 1943) and Matilde. He seems to have been capable of being passionately in love with two women at the same time. When confronted by Delia in 1955 and asked to choose between her and Matilde, he found this impossible. Indeed, he tearfully begged Delia to stay with him during a meeting with Galo González, the secretary-general of the Chilean Communist Party, who was anxious to avoid a public scandal. Delia refused: 'This is not a bourgeois marriage, Pablo. If there's no love, there's no marriage.'

Anyone reading *Las uvas y el viento*, therefore, should be aware not only of Neruda's commitment to the burgeoning Socialist republics of Central and Eastern Europe but his knowledge that his love for Matilde could, and probably would, eventually cause the disintegration of his relationship with Delia, which had lasted twenty years. These twin sensations – of new beginnings and the ending of an era – cannot be underplayed.

'Sólo el hombre' (Only Man, p. 79) is, in a sense, another version of his humanist hymn, 'The Fugitive (1948),' from his 1950 epic, *Canto general*, about the generosity of the strangers who had been harbouring him in hiding. Interestingly, however, unlike in that previous poem, the natural world is for once seen here as hostile, rather than as an ally. And here, one man becomes fellow man, all of mankind. 'Palabras a Europa' (Words for Europe, p. 83) is evidently the closest to Socialist realism of the poems that I have chosen from *Las uvas y el viento*. But it is tempered by tenderness. 'Caballera de Capri' (Tangle of Capri Hair, p. 85) and 'La pasajera de Capri' (Passenger on Capri, p. 93) are love songs – both to Capri and to Matilde, with whom he shared an idyll of several months on the island in 1952, before returning to Chile from exile. One of the earliest biographies of Neruda was Emir Rodríguez Monegal's *El viajero inmóvil* (The Immobile Voyager), published in 1966. It is an apt title. Neruda did indeed travel the world, but he was motionless in the sense that wherever he went, his heart remained fixed on Chile. This longing is touchingly depicted in 'Cuándo de Chile?' (When, Chile?, p. 99)

'Un día' (This Day, p. 107) is another love poem with much of the direct simplicity of some of the other love poems Neruda wrote in the 1950s, especially those in *Los versos del capitán* (The Captain's Verses, 1952) or the very moving final section of *Estravagario* (Extravagaria, 1958). In stark contrast, 'Londres' (London, p. 111) is an extraordinarily bitter poem, full of bile towards the British Government (the Labour Government of Clement Attlee) for refusing him entry to the United Kingdom in 1950 to attend the World Peace Congress in Sheffield. The British authorities considered the congress to be a Communist front.

Published in December 1967, *La barcarola* (Waterboat Song) is largely an extended love poem to Matilde. It is also one of the most surreal books Neruda produced in later years In a poem like 'Resurecciones' (Resurrections), for example, which I have not included in this edition, he writes: 'Friend, it's your kiss that sings like a bell in the water of the submerged cathedral, through whose window entered eyeless fish, dissolute seaweed…' But Dominic Moran also calls *La barcarola* 'a virtuoso experiment in versification in honour of Rubén Darío.'[36] It was published on the centenary of Darío's birth, and Darío portrayed himself as an amorous gondolier in the first poem in his 1905 collection, *Cantos de vida y esperanza* (Songs of Life and Hope). I have pointed out elsewhere that Neruda's debt to Darío lasted throughout his life.[37] The intriguing reference to the 'guitar-coloured wind' in 'Sonata' (p. 124) from *La barcarola* is reminiscent of Neruda's surprising allusions to violins in many poems throughout his life – for example, the 'violin-coloured insect' in *Tentativa del hombre infinito* – but Darío also frequently used violins in seemingly incongruous contexts.

'Primavera en Chile' (Spring in Chile, p. 127) is an intoxicating sensory delight, and notice how Neruda obstinately repeats that word 'roots' in 'Pucatrihue' (p. 129), at one point addressing Delia (who, it will be recalled, had cautioned against its excessive use) directly. This could be seen as either impish or insensitive on Neruda's part, bearing in mind that Neruda had finally married Matilde the year before he published *La barcarola*, and was now firmly wedded to Chile. Except that this Delia is not his former wife, at all, but his Chilean writer friend, Delia Domínguez.

Neruda's astounding late burst of energy produced *La espada encendida* (The Flaming Sword), published in Buenos Aires by Losada in September 1970. It was written over the period of the preceding year, coinciding with Neruda's Presidential candidature for the Communist Party and his eventual withdrawal in favour of the Socialist, Salvador Allende. The book, which consists of eighty-seven poems, tells the post-apocalyptical tale of Rhodo, a 130-year-old fugitive from the last wars on earth who has escaped to Patagonia, in southern Chile, to establish a solitary kingdom of one man now that all human life has ended and who falls in with a young girl, Rosía. Their passion overcomes the

[36] Moran, *op. cit.*, p. 168
[37] In 'Rubén Darío y Pablo Neruda: Los paralelos posibles', the lecture which I presented at the Universidad Nacional Autónoma de Nicaragua (UNAN) in León, Nicaragua on 20 February 2019

hostile territory as well as the fire of the volcano threatening their very existence. At first sight, it might appear as though Neruda was reassessing some of the central Christian explanations of the Creation, with the volcano representing the swords of fire placed at the entrance to the Garden of Eden when Adam and Eve were expelled from Paradise. Indeed, Enrico Mario Santí has called *La espada encendida* a re-writing of *Canto general*, 'an explicit apocalypse as well as his [Neruda's] last prophetic book.'[38] In fact, the initial idea for *La espada encendida* appears to have come from 'L'incendie terrestre' (The Earthly Conflagration) – a short prose poem by the French symbolist writer, Marcel Schwob, which Neruda had translated into Spanish for *Claridad* back in 1923 – depicting a final catastrophe of the planet similar to a natural disaster caused by climatic change brought about by moral corruption. That, at least, is Hernán Loyola's contention.[39] Neruda had also translated Schwob's short story, *Le roi au masque d'or* (The King with the Golden Mask), into Spanish in 1923.

Frank Riess has also intriguingly suggested that a 'guiding thread' in the story may be the work of William Blake. Neruda's translations of two Blake poems – 'Visions of the Daughters of Albion' and 'The Mental Traveller' – had appeared in the Spanish magazine, *Cruz y Raya*, in Madrid in 1934. Riess believes that the play of three elements – earth, water and fire – in *La espada encendida* and the movement from earth to water have links to Blake's vision. The fire in both authors' works, according to Riess, is 'the light or wisdom of the soul buried inside the earth to forge minerals below.'[40]

However, we now know that there was a more personal story behind *La espada encendida*: namely, Neruda's final love affair, at the age of 65, with Matilde's niece, Alicia Urrutia. (Matilde had invited Alicia to stay with them at Isla Negra with Alicia's young daughter, Rosario, the name Neruda

---

[38] Enrico Mario Santí: *The Poetics of Prophesy* (New York: Cornell University Press.1982), p. 182
[39] See Pablo Neruda: *Obras completas, op. cit.*, Vol. 3, p. 980
[40] See *Cantalao*, Vol. 2, 2014, p. 45

had initially given to Matilde to disguise their relationship.) The'fugitive' Rhodo is Neruda himself and Alicia was the direct inspiration for Rosía. The erotic, tender and sometimes brutal, power of the passages I have selected for this edition are undeniable. Indeed, the strength of Neruda's passion was such that it threatened to destroy his marriage to Matilde. This was the reason he asked Salvador Allende to appoint him Ambassador to France – to ensure some geographical distance was forged between himself and Alicia. Nevertheless, we now know that Alicia kept writing equally impassioned letters to Neruda in Paris (via his second-in-command there, Jorge Edwards).

Osvaldo Rodríguez has noted that ever since Neruda's initial encounter with Quevedo, his poetry had acquired a progressively greater ethical dimension until, by the late and posthumous poetry, 'it cast doubt on any sign of personal vanity or arrogance.[41] *Geografía infructuosa* (Fruitless Geography), published by Losada in 1972, has some of the same combination of delightful, self-deprecating humour and a darker awareness of his own mortality that run through one of my own favourites of all Neruda's books, *Estravagario*, which appeared fourteen years earlier (when he did not yet have cancer but suffered from frequent bouts of phlebitis, a painful swelling of the legs). But more than his own mortality, *Geografía infructuosa* is concerned with humanity's fragility.

'El cobarde' (The Coward, p. 147) was probably written in the spring of 1972 at La Manquel, the house at Condé-sur-Iton, in Normandy, northern France, which Neruda bought with the winnings from the previous year's Nobel Prize. Note how his own very specific physical pain fuses with the world's agony:

a single petal from the vast human hurt
falls into your urine and it seems as though
the whole world's bleeding dry.

Incitación al Nixonicidio y Alabanza de la Revolución Chilena

[41] See Osvaldo Rodríguez (undated lecture): 'La poesía póstuma de Pablo Neruda: viaje al interior de sí mismo'

(Incitement to Nixonicide and Praise for the Chilean Revolution) was the last of Neruda's books to be published in his lifetime. He wrote it in Chile in a mere two months, between December 1972 and January 1973, just after returning home on giving up his post as Ambassador to France through illness. It was printed in February 1973 by the Santiago publishers, Quimantú, in a special 1,000-copy run. (A larger edition came out the following month in the Peruvian capital, Lima, published by Grijalbo.) It is a book full of anxiety about his country's future. And he had a lot to be worried about. He feared (correctly, as it turned out) that Chile was moving in the same direction as Spain in the mid-1930s, heading for a civil war in which the far Right would prove victorious. The Popular Unity coalition of Salvador Allende, who had become the first democratically elected Marxist head of state on 4 September 1970, was coming under increasing pressure from US-backed opposition forces: President Richard Nixon and his Secretary of State, Henry Kissinger, were determined to do everything in their power not to allow Chile to go the same way as Cuba.

The book was heavily criticised for placing blatant polemic above love and lyricism. Dominic Moran, for example, has called it 'a barrage of rhymed insults and incriminations, sporadically leavened by a stanza or two in support of the Allende regime.'[42] Some of these criticisms are perhaps a little over-simplistic. Of course the book contains a great deal of pamphleteering. Neruda himself said in the prologue that he saw no option but to write what he called 'an attack on the enemies of my people, [an attack] as hard as Araucanian stone... So stand firm. I'm about to fire the first shot!' But he also intended to envelop the bullets in a love poem or two to his embattled nation.

One of those love-wrapped bullets was 'Aquí me quedo' (I'm Here to Stay, p. 149), an anthem to human solidarity and unity. It is certainly lyrical, and indeed the poem was wonderfully set to music by the Chilean singer-songwriter, Víctor Jara, not long after its publication. Jara himself was murdered by the military junta on 16 September 1973.

---

[42] Moran, *op. cit.*, p. 187

Neruda learned of the killing while lying gravely ill in hospital in Santiago. 'That's like killing a nightingale,' Neruda reportedly exclaimed when he heard the news. It was a comment with poignant echoes of his description of his great Spanish poet friend, Miguel Hernández, who had died of tuberculosis in prison in Franco's Spain back in 1943.

President Allende intended to organise a nationwide celebration on 12 July 1974 to mark Neruda's seventieth birthday. And the poet himself planned to present a literary gift to the world: seven books of verse and his *Memoirs*. Neither man lived to see 1974. Allende committed suicide on 11 September 1973, the day of Augusto Pinochet's military coup. Neruda died just twelve days later.

Losada brought out all eight books posthumously in 1974 They included some magnificent late lyrical poems, as well as the witty, mischievously surreal couplets of *Libro de preguntas* (Book of Questions) and some of the very last poems he ever wrote, in *El mar y las campanas* (The Sea and the Bells), which Dominic Moran astutely asserts are replete with lines of 'limpid tranquillity'.[43] Jaime Alazraki maintains that the cyclical shape, reminiscent of Brahmin philosophy, in many of these late poems belies Neruda own claims to have been unmoved – or even alienated – by the Eastern religions he countered while serving as consul in the Far East. This is an intriguing, if ultimately unconvincing view, although Neruda is undoubtedly withdrawing within himself in many of these final books, in a way he had rejected after his experiences in 1930s Spain.

To close this edition, I have selected poems from two of Neruda's posthumous collections, *Elegía* (Elegy) and *Defectos escogidos* (Chosen Defects).

In *Elegía*, Neruda changed tone once again, for even in ill-health, his drive for re-invention remained intact. It is a largely sombre collection in which he bids farewell to Moscow, the city he had loved ever since he first visited it in 1949 for the one hundred and fiftieth anniversary of the birth of Alexander Pushkin. The book pays tribute to many friends who had died in the Soviet capital, including Ilya

[43] Moran, *op. cit.*, p. 193

Ehrenburg, the Spanish sculptor Alberto Sánchez, the Turkish poet Nazim Hikmet, and the Soviet poet Simion Kirsanov. In fact, the book emerged from a genuine trip Neruda made with Matilde from Paris to Moscow in December 1971, in the hope that Soviet doctors could halt the advance of the cancer which would soon force him to renounce his Ambassadorship in Paris. As Osvaldo Rodríguez has pointed out, it is a book not only about the loss of Russian friends but about his own increasing loneliness – that same nagging solitude which he had fled, first, by abandoning Temuco for Santiago, then by leaving the Far East for Buenos Aires, but which, inevitably, he could no longer forestall as the deaths of so many companions took its toll.[44]

In some ways, *Elegía* is most notable for voicing explicit doubts about Stalin and Stalinism. In his 1969 collection, *Fin de mundo* (End of the World), Neruda had expressed his sense of shock over the crushing of the Prague Spring by Soviet tanks the previous year ('The hour of Prague fell / on my head like a stone') and in 1971, he had told a French journalist: 'We were wrong.' Yet at the end of his life, he could still not bring himself to condemn Stalin entirely. In *Elegía*, he describes Stalin as being caught between God and the Devil yet mysteriously, perhaps sentimentally, Neruda refers to him as 'that wise, tranquil Georgian / an expert on wine and many other things.'

It is not true, however, as some critics have claimed, that *Elegía* lacks any trace of humour or irony. To illustrate my point, I have selected the poem Neruda dedicated to the Soviet poet, Yevgeny Yevtushenko. The two men had a complicated relationship. They did not always see eye to eye politically but Neruda admired – and perhaps secretly envied – his Soviet friend's ability and readiness to speak out freely against the official line. Neruda's fascinating reference to the two of them as 'clowns' in this poem unwittingly reveals these tensions and complexities. For Neruda and Yevtushenko were both showmen, conscious of their fame and of being the centre of attention, just as clowns are. But while Neruda calls for them to join forces and use poetry

[44] See Osvaldo Rodríguez (undated lecture), *op. cit.*

so that the truth will beam out
once again
from among the shadows.

Clowns also mask their true identity behind a disguise. And is the world as organised as a circus, or full of people playing child-like games?

Yevtushenko, whom I knew, was a close friend of my mother, the poet Elaine Feinstein. She recalled a wonderful anecdote he told her about one of Neruda's many trips to Moscow. During a visit to Yevgeny's apartment, Neruda suddenly announced: 'I have to go. I have an important dinner'. A couple of hours later, there was a knock at Yevtushenko's door. It was Neruda again. Mildly surprised, Yevgeny asked him whether he had enjoyed the dinner. 'Dinner? What dinner? I've been stuck in your lift for the past two hours!'

Just days after Neruda's death, Yevtushenko wrote a profoundly touching 'Epistle' in which he declared that the Chilean 'carries his poetry to the people / as simply and calmly / as a loaf of bread.'[45] This poem, incidentally, appeared in a collection called *The Face Behind the Face,* a title which curiously recalls that possible theme of masking in Neruda's own poem to Yevtushenko.

Despite that clown-showman image mentioned above, the very title of the other posthumous collection I have chosen to feature, *Chosen Defects,* bears testimony to Neruda's humility in the face of the inevitable. Uncertainty over his fate has now become a reality. *Defectos escogidos* marks a return to the attractive self-mockery of *Estravagario.* But ill-health hangs over it.

'Parodia del guerrero' (The Warrior's Parody, p. 157) is a startling poem. Neruda sounds almost delirious as he perceives his gout-ridden legs as useless. His clumsy feet are independent from the rest of his body – rather like his legs in a poem from forty years earlier, 'Ritual de mis piernas' (Ritual of My Legs), in *Residence on Earth.* But this late poem has a

[45] Yevgeny Yevtushenko: 'Epistle to Neruda' in *The Face Behind the Face,* trans. Arthur Boyars and Simon Franklin. (London: Marion Boyars, 1979)

darker, more cosmic significance. As Osvaldo Rodríguez has written: 'In the poetic fiction of "The Warrior's Parody", the already "fossilised" subject approaches the abyss of death to dive into the well when lives are submerged and ask those who have already gone, with apparent innocence: "And what are you doing down there?"'[46]

Journeys had been a theme of Neruda's poetry all his life. But for a poet who did not believe in transcendence, death (despite the lessons he had learned from Quevedo – and he entitled a magnificent poem 'With Quevedo, in Spring' in another collection published posthumously, *Jardín de invierno* – Winter Garden), was the final journey. It was an unwanted one from which there could be no return. Yet, just like his adolescent self in Temuco, he valiantly refuses to surrender entirely to despair. Listen to the pathos mingling with defiance at the end of the bitingly satirical 'El gran orinador' (The Great Urinator, p. 161).

Indeed, as it turned out, death was not the final journey, after all. Neruda's body was exhumed on 8 April 2013 – by an odd coincidence, the same day Margaret Thatcher died – in an attempt to determine whether he had been poisoned by his political enemies in the Santiago hospital where he was being treated for cancer. His remains were sent to forensic scientists in four countries but, at the time of writing, with Neruda now re-buried alongside his third wife, Matilde Urrutia, at his Pacific Coast house at Isla Negra, no conclusive results have been announced one way or the other. How Neruda, that passionate reader of thrillers, would have loved this intrigue – if he had not been at the centre of it! And I have the feeling that Quevedo would have laughed along with him.

Adam Feinstein

---

[46] See Osvaldo Rodríguez (undated lecture): 'El motivo del viaje en la poesía póstuma de Pablo Neruda'

THE UNKNOWN NERUDA

LO ESTÉRIL

Adentro de mi vida voy echando mi ensueño
en lloviznas sutiles de amor y de veneno.

Me fecundó el abismo, se deshizo mi encanto
y en el dolor quedéme dolorido pensando.

(Era un canto adormido
en seda triste y blanda,
se adurmió en el estéril desgarrón de los vientos
y la vida, hecha trizas como un árbol desierto
quedó.)

Oh! Duelen, duelen y duelen los dolores humildes!

[1919]

EN LA VENTANA

Ayer, ayer no más, como una carga
era mi corazón un ritmo bueno.

Y no pasó una amada,
no pasó un canto amable florecido de ensueño.

No pasó una alborada.
No pasaron los pájaros trinadores de luz.
No pasó nada, nada.

(Los hombres se callaban. Yo miraba el azul,
pasó una nube rubia, pero nunca volvió.)

STERILITY

My life is a daydream of
fine drizzle, love and poison.

My delight was dismantled in the fertile abyss
and there I stood, suffering in the agony of thought.

(It was a drowsy song
draped in sad, soft silk,
slumbering in the sterile gash of the wind
and life clung on, in shreds, like
an abandoned tree.)

Oh, the pain, the pain, the pain of humble pain!

AT THE WINDOW

Yesterday, just a day ago, my heart
throbbed to a happy beat, like a charge

yet no lover strolled by, it seems,
no song, no tender blossoming of dreams

no dawn walked past
no birds trilling with the light
no thrills, nothing.

(The people said not a word. I gazed out at the blue,
at a passing cloud, a blonde never to return.)

(A qué mundo? A qué mundo
te fuiste, nube rubia, candorosa y cobarde?)

Ir viviendo, Señor! como un milagro
dormido en los cansancios de la tarde.

   [1920]

NO SEAS COMO EL ÁRBOL PRIMIFLORO

No seas como el árbol primifloro
que después de dar hojas y morirse
comienza a florecer.
                    La vida tuya
necesita de tierra removida
germinadora y buena. Todo paso
de otoños ha de ser como una ruta
que te alumbre de sol las yemas nuevas.
Después arder, hundirse en el espasmo
de florecer y florecer...
                    Más tarde
la primavera pasará cantando...

   [1920]

(Where were you heading, my blonde,
innocent, cowardly cloud? To another world?)

My God, it's such a miracle to be alive,
dozing in the languor of late evening.

THE FIRST FLOWERS*

Do not mimic the tree
that grows leaves, then dies
before the first flowers appear.
                              Your life
needs a restless soil
for goodness to grow. Every passing
autumn paves a sunlit path to new buds
and blazes. And then you subside
in a spasm of blossom.
                    Until
another spring wanders by, humming.

* This was the first poem Neftalí Reyes signed under his pseudonym,
Pablo Neruda

PRIMAVERA

La lluvia cae, payasos,
sobre las calles mojadas.
Ojos que nada miraron,
boca que no dijo nada.
(Oh Primavera de grumos
dulces, de carnes rosadas,
cielos de un azul obscuro
y aguas de color de agua.
Ahora
carmín sobre bocas muertas,
broma,
fiesta.
Para quién llegaste, para
quién llegaste, Primavera?

[1920]

LUNA

Cuando nací mi madre se moría
con una santidad de ánima en pena.
Era su cuerpo transparente. Ella tenía
bajo la carne un luminar de estrellas.
Ella murió. Yo nací.
                    Por eso llevo
un invisible río entre las venas,
un invencible canto de crepúsculo
que me enciende la risa y me la hiela.
Ella juntó a la vida que nacía
su estéril ramazón de vida enferma.

A NEW SPRING

You clowns, can't you see
the rain falling on damp streets?
Your eyes saw nothing,
your mouths said nothing.
(Spring, with its sweet,
pink clots of flesh
and dark blue skies
and water-coloured water.)
Now
carmine over dead mouths,
mirth,
party time.
So who was waiting for you,
spring, when you arrived?

MOON

When she gave birth to me, my mother was
already dying, in pain, with the soul of a saint.
Her body was transparent.
The stars glittered beneath her skin.
She died. I was born.
                    That's why
an invisible river courses through my veins:
an unbreakable song of twilight ignites my laughter,
only to douse it in ice.
To the launch of my life
she added the sterile tangle
of sick mortality.

43

El marfil de sus manos moribundas
tornó amarilla en mí la luna llena…
Por eso – hermano – está tan triste el campo
detrás de las vidrieras transparentes…
Esta luna amarilla de mi vida
me hace ser un retorno de la muerte.

[1922]

PALABRAS DE AMOR

En la noche de estrellas te he besado las manos…

Piensa, yo que te he visto perdida y recobrada;
piensa, yo que me alejo de ti cuando me esperas;
piensa, esta dolorosa paz del campo dormido
oloroso a las flores y a las frutas primeras…

Todo lo sabes, todo. Lo has escuchado todo
con los inmensos ojos perdidos a lo lejos;
cuando callo me miras y de mi boca cae
como una flor cortada para tu boca un beso.

(Ésta es la despedida cuando apenas llegaba,
esto es tocar apenas los puertos y partir…
Que me amarren tus brazos, que no me dejen irme
para tocar apenas otro amor y partir!)

Tú escuchas mis palabras ye recoges mis besos,
y prolongamos juntos el silencio del campo
rayado por el duro ladrido de los perros
y por la numerosa canción de nuestros pasos.
… En la noche de estrellas te he besado las manos…

The moribund marble of her hands
dyed the full moon yellow.
That's why, my brother, the land looks so sad through the
    clear window...
This yellow moon casts me as the offshoot of death.

WORDS OF LOVE

I kissed your hands on a starry night.

Think: I who have seen you lost and found;
think: I who shrink away as you wait for me;
think: the fields slumbering in the pain of peace,
the scent of flowers and premature fruit.

You know everything, everything. You've heard it all
with your huge eyes staring into the distance.
When I'm silent, you gaze at me and my mouth droops
like a flower plucked as a kiss for your lips.

(So it's already time for farewells –
We've only just arrived and we must leave again ...
Wrap me in the anchor of your arms, don't let me go
to another love, to yet another parting.)

You hear my words, gather up my kisses,
and we share the silent expanse of the fields,
broken only by the grating barks of dogs
and the countless songs of our footsteps.
I kissed your hands on a starry night.

Cruzo de despedida tu amor y me detienes.
Voy a decirte adiós y me queman tus ojos;
te voy a dar la angustia que golpea mis sienes
y galopa en mis venas como centauro loco,

pero mi voz se ha vuelto cantarina y ardiente
y mis dedos revuelven tu cabellera oscura;
en la noche de estrellas mis palabras se pierden
y caminamos ebrios de la misma dulzura.
... Todo lo sabes, todo. Lo has escuchado apenas,
pero lo sabes todo.

[1922]

As we say farewell to love, I meet you one more time.
You stop me. Your eyes scorch as I try to say goodbye.
I planned to give you the torment throbbing in my temples,
the crazed centaur of agony galloping through my veins.

But my voice is suddenly ablaze with melody
and my fingers caress the black threads of your hair.
My words fade into the starry night
and we walk together, drunk on our sweet union.

You know everything, everything. You scarcely heard
a word, but you know everything.

de
CREPUSCULARIO
(1923)

MORENA, LA BESADORA

Cabellera rubia, suelta,
corriendo como un estero,
cabellera.

Uñas duras y doradas,
flores curvas y sensuales,
uñas duras y doradas.

Comba del vientre, escondida,
y abierta como una fruta
o una herida.

Dulce rodilla desnuda
apretada en mis rodillas,
dulce rodilla desnuda.

Enredadera del pelo
entre la oferta redonda
de los senos.

Huella que dura en el lecho,
huella dormida en el alma,
palabras locas.

Perdidas palabras locas:
rematarán mis canciones,
se morirán nuestras bocas.

Morena, la Besadora,
rosal de todas las rosas
en una hora.

from
CREPUSCULARIO
(1923)

KISS ME, MY DARK-SKINNED ONE

Your hair runs loose and
blonde as a brook,
your hair.

Your hard, golden nails
sensual as flowers' curves,
hard, golden nails.

The warp of your stomach, hidden
or exposed like a fruit
or a wound.

Your soft naked knee
pressing against my knees,
soft naked knee.

A tangle of hair
between the rounded gift
of your breasts.

The trace of you lingers in the bed,
asleep in my soul,
wild words.

Wild words, stray words,
rounding off my songs:
our mouths will die together.

Kiss me, my dark-skinned one,
gather a whole rosebush
in just an hour.

Besadora dulce y rubia,
me iré,
te irás, Besadora.

Pero aún tengo la aurora
enredada en cada sien.

Bésame, por eso, ahora,
bésame, Besadora,
ahora y en la hora
de nuestra muerte.

Amén.

FAREWELL

1.

Desde el fondo de ti, y arrodillado,
un niño triste, como yo, nos mira.

Por esa vida que arderá en sus venas
tendrían que amarrarse nuestras vidas.

Por esas manos, hijas de tus manos,
tendrían que matar las manos mías.

Por sus ojos abiertos en la tierra
veré en los tuyos lágrimas un día.

Kiss me, my sweet blonde-haired one.
I will go,
you will go. Kiss me.

But my temples are still
tangled in the dawn.

So kiss me now,
kiss me, you who have kissed
so many times before.
Do it now and every hour
until we die.

Amen.

FAREWELL

1.

Deep within you, a sad child
just like me kneels and stares at us.

Our lives will be anchored
to the life coursing through his veins.

For his hands, daughters of your hands,
my own hands would have to die.

For his eyes, gazing wide open at the earth,
your eyes will fill with tears one day.

2.

Yo no lo quiero, Amada.

Para que nada nos amarre
que no nos una nada.

Ni la palabra que aromó tu boca,
ni lo que no dijeron las palabras.

Ni la fiesta de amor que no tuvimos,
ni tus sollozos junto a la ventana.

3.

(Amo el amor de los marineros
que besan y se van.

Dejan una promesa.
No vuelven nunca más.

En cada puerto una mujer espera:
los marineros besan y se van.

Una noche se acuestan con la muerte
en el lecho del mar).

4.

Amo el amor que se reparte
en besos, lecho y pan.

Amor que puede ser eterno
y puede ser fugaz.

2.

My darling, I don't love him.

There must be no anchor,
nothing to tether us.

Nothing. Not the scent of a word on your lips,
nor anything left unsaid.

Not the festival of love we never celebrated,
nor your sobs at the window.

3.

(I love the love of sailors
who kiss and then vanish,

leave promises behind
but never return.

There's a woman waiting in every port:
sailors kiss and then vanish.

And one night, they make love
to death on the sea bed.

4.

I love the love that's offered up
in bed, with kisses and bread.

A love that can last for ever
or no more than an instant.

53

Amor que quiere libertarse
para volver a amar.

Amor divinizado que se acerca
Amor divinizado que se va.

5.

Ya no se encantarán mis ojos en tus ojos,
ya no se endulzará junto a ti mi dolor.

Pero hacia donde vaya llevaré tu mirada
y hacia donde camines llevarás mi dolor.

Fui tuyo, fuiste mía. Qué más? Juntos hicimos
un recodo en la ruta donde el amor pasó.

Fui tuyo, fuiste mía. Tú serás del que te ame,
del que corte en tu huerto lo que he sembrado yo.

Yo me voy. Estoy triste: pero siempre estoy triste.
Vengo desde tus brazos. No sé hacia dónde voy.

… Desde tu corazón me dice adiós un niño.
Y yo le digo adiós.

A love that craves the freedom
to love all over again.

A divine love that sweeps in,
another that slips away.)

    5.

My eyes will no longer be bewitched by yours.
My pain will no longer be sweetened beside you.

But I will remember your eyes wherever I go
and you will carry my pain wherever you go.

I was yours, you were mine. What else? Together,
we stopped to make love at a bend in the road.

I was yours, you were mine. You'll belong to another.
I planted the seed and he'll cut down the tree.

I must go. I'm sad – but then I'm always sad.
I pull myself away from your arms. But where will I go?

From the depth of your heart, a child waves farewell.
I wave back. Farewell.

EL PADRE

Tierra de sembradura inculta y brava,
tierra en que no hay esteros ni caminos,
mi vida bajo el sol tiembla y se alarga.

Padre, tus ojos dulces nada pueden,
como nada pudieron las estrellas
que me abrasan los ojos y las sienes.

El mal de amor me enceguerió la vista
y en la fontana dulce de mi sueño
se reflejó otra fuente estremecida.

Después… Pregunta a Dios por qué me dieron
lo que me dieron y por qué después
supe una soledad de tierra y cielo.

Mira, mi juventud fue un brote puro
que se quedó sin estallar y pierde
su dulzura de sangres y de jugos.

El sol que cae y cae eternamente
se cansó de besarla… Y el otoño.
Padre, tus ojos dulces nada pueden.

Escucharé en la noche tus palabras:
… niño, mi niño…
Y en la noche inmensa
seguiré con mis llagas y tus llagas

FATHER

Savage soil, barren and unsown,
land without brooks or tracks,
where my life stretches out and quivers.

Father, your gentle eyes can do nothing.
Nor can the stars, scorching
my eyes and my temples.

I was blinded by the sickness of love
and in the sweet fountain of sleep,
another spring now trembles.

And then... Ask God why I was given
gifts and then came to know
this solitude, both earthly and heavenly.

Look, my boyhood was a pure bud
which never flowered and shed
all its sweet blood and juices.

The sun falls and falls again and for ever,
tires of kissing her... and then the autumn comes.
Father, your gentle eyes can do nothing.

I will hear your voice in the night:
Son, my son...
And in the immense night,
I will live with my wounds and yours.

BARRIO SIN LUZ

Se va la poesía de las cosas
o no la puede condensar mi vida?
Ayer – mirando el último crepúsculo –
yo era un manchón de musgo entre una ruinas.

Las ciudades – hollines y venganzas –
la cochinada gris de los suburbios,
la oficina que encorva las espaldas,
el jefe de ojos turbios.

Sangre de un arrebol sobre los cerros,
sangre sobre las calles y las plazas,
dolor de corazones rotos,
podre de hastíos y de lágrimas.

Un río abraza el arrabal como una
mano helada que tienta en las tinieblas:
sobre sus aguas
se avergüenzan de verse las estrellas.

Y las casas que esconden los deseos
detrás de las ventanas luminosas,
mientras afuera el viento
lleva un poco de barro a cada rosa.

Lejos… la bruma de las olvidanzas
– humos espesos, tajamares rotos –,
y el campo, el campo verde!, en que jadean
los bueyes y los hombres sudorosos.

Y aquí estoy yo, brotado entre las ruinas,
mordiendo solo todas las tristezas,
como si el llanto fuera una semilla
y yo el único surco de la tierra.

SUBURBAN GLOOM

The poetry of things slips away:
can't my life hold it back?
Yesterday, watching the final glimmers of dusk,
I was a mossy stain among the ruins.

City of soot and vengeance,
the grim, grey filth of the suburbs,
workers hunched in offices,
under their bosses' turbid glare.

Red clouds bleeding over hills,
over streets, over squares,
the pain of broken hearts,
pus of ennui and tears.

A river hugs the dismal outskirts like an
icy hand fondling the shadows:
even the stars are ashamed
of their reflections in the water.

And the houses hiding desires
behind their glowing windows
while outside, the wind
covers the roses in mud.

Far away… The fog of oblivion
– thick fumes, shattered wharfs –
and the fields, the green fields, where
oxen pant and men sweat.

And here am I, emerging from the ruins,
alone, gnawing at any sadness that passes,
as if my sobs were seeds
and I were the only furrow in the ground.

MAESTRANZAS DE NOCHE

Hierro negro que duerme, fierro negro que gime
por cada poro un grito de desconsolación.

Las cenizas ardidas sobre la tierra triste,
los caldos en que el bronce derritió su dolor.

Aves de qué lejano país desventurado
graznaron en la noche dolorosa y sin fin?

Y el grito se me crispa como un nervio enroscado
o como la cuerda rota de un violín.

Cada máquina tiene una pupila abierta
para mirarme a mí.

En las paredes cuelgan las interrogaciones,
florece en las bigornias el alma de los bronces
y hay un temblor de pasos en los cuartos desiertos.

Y entre la noche negra – desesperadas – corren
y sollozan las almas de los obreros muertos.

WORKSHOPS AT NIGHT

The black iron sleeps, the black iron groans,
a desolate howl from every pore.

Ashes smarting on the sad ground,
cauldrons of bronze melting in pain.

From which ill-fated country were the birds
that caw in the sorrows of an endless night?

The screams make me wince like a coiled nerve
or the snapped string of a violin.

Each machine keeps one eye open
to stare at me.

Questions hang on the walls,
metal souls blossom on the anvils
and I hear a tremble of footsteps in deserted rooms.

And in the blackness of night, the souls
of dead workers race and sob in despair.

Ésta es mi casa
aún la perfuman los bosques
desde donde la acarreaban
allí tricé mi corazón como el espejo para andar a través de
    mí mismo
ésa es la alta ventana y ahí quedan las puertas
de quién fue el hacha que rompió los troncos
tal vez el viento colgó de las vigas
su peso profundo olvidándolo entonces
era cuando la noche bailaba entre sus redes
cuando el niño despertó sollozando
yo no cuento yo digo en palabras desgraciadas
aún los andamios dividen el crepúsculo
y detrás de los vidrios la luz del petróleo
era para mirar hacia el cielo
caía la lluvia en pétalos de vidrio
ahí seguiste el camino que iba a la tempestad
como las altas insistencias del mar
aíslan las piedras duras de las orillas del aire
qué quisiste qué ponías como muriendo muchas veces
todas las cosas suben a un gran silencio
y él se desesperaba inclinado en su borde
sostenías una flor dolorosa
entre sus pétalos giraban los días margaritas de pilotos decaídos
decaído desocupado revolviste de la sombra
el metal de las últimas distancias o esperabas el turno
amaneció sin embargo en los relojes de la tierra
de pronto los días trepan a los años
he aquí tu corazón andando estás cansado sosteniéndote
a tu lado se despiden los pájaros de la estación ausente

from
ENDEAVOUR OF THE INFINITE MAN
(1926)

This is my house
still perfumed by the forests
that built it
this was where my heart shattered like a mirror and I walked
    through myself
and there's the high window and the doors
whose was the axe that hacked down trunks
perhaps the wind left its weighty bulk
dangling from the rafters and forgot it there
as the night danced in its nets
and the little boy woke up sobbing
I'm not telling this right just using unfortunate words
dawn is still scaffolded in two
and from behind the window the oil light
gazed out at the sky
the rain fell in glass petals
and you headed towards the storm
as the lofty urgings of the sea
unfasten the firm stone from the lips of the air
what did you want what were you wearing as if dying
    again and again
everything leads to total silence
and he was on the edge hunched in despair
you were holding a sorry flower
through its petals flitted days marguerites of downcast flyers
and you too were crestfallen vacant but you unsettled
the steel in the last distant darkness or waited your turn
dawn still stirred on the clock faces of the earth
and suddenly days climb over years
your heart wanders you're tired you hold yourself up
and beside you birds wave from an absent station

ODA TÓRRIDA

Venid con vuestro cargamento de direcciones rojas,
veranos duros, permanentes, agrios de estas zonas de la tierra,
cargad sobre mis sienes sacos de sudor blanco,
cegadme de luz loca, de relámpagos viejos,
heridme el corazón con vuestros besos de brasa y vidrio,
entrad en mis materias intestinales, mordiendo
mi blando ser interior con alimentos devoradores,
pimienta, ají, jengibre, marisco, nueces ardientes,
alimentos que atenazan como cangrejos y aún
corred, zona infinita, vuestras influencias líquidas,
en mi garganta extrañamente exasperada,
vuestros espesos manantiales de azúcar,
vuestros infinitos espermas, oh tierra creadora de la vida,
vuestros petróleos sutiles mezclados a la orina de las bestias
     salvajes,
el barro apocalíptico de los búfalos y el lodo fino de los
     arrozales,
el té y lluvia del monzón y el rocío entre las orquídeas,
oh tierra de los infiernos reunidos,
cielo mío,
junta desde luego tus sólidos en mi alma,
tu suelo exorbitante y tenaz,
tus piedras capaces de nutrir, y aun
la raíz de tus minerales, la piel y el cuero de tus bestias,
las uñas y el pico de tus vivientes pájaros,
la sed de tus instrumentos, el sonido
oscuro, turbador del trueno en tu cielo,
tu lento vital silencio como alcohol o ácido,
y tus cifras secretas de muerte y permanencia
entierra en las pasajeras tierras de mi alma.

   [1931]

TORRID ODE

Come here with your cargo of red-scrawled addresses,
your harsh, ever-lasting summers, bitter summers of these parts,
pile your sacks of white sweat high on my temples,
blind me with your crazy glow, your ancient lightning,
knife my heart with your blazing coal and shards of glass,
Burrow deep into my intestines, gnaw away at
my soft insides with your devastating delicacies:
peppers, chillies, ginger, shellfish, nuts that scorch,
food that grips as tight as crabs and,
in a limitless expanse, your liquid influence flows
down my oddly exasperated gullet,
thick streams of sugar,
infinite sperm in its creative soil of life,
your subtle petroleum mixed with the urine of wild animals,
the apocalyptic buffalo mud and the delicate slime of the rice fields,
the tea and rain from the monsoons and the dew drenching the
    orchids,
oh, land of joined-up hells,
my sky,
feel free to reunite your solids in my soul,
your stubborn, exorbitant soil,
your nutritious stones and even
your mineral roots, the hide and leather of your beasts,
the fingernails and beaks of birds,
your thirsting instruments, the
obscure, distressing sound of thunder in the sky,
your slow silence, as vital as alcohol or acid,
and your secret statistics of death and permanence,
buried in the passing territories of my soul.

NÚMERO Y NOMBRE

De un sueño al sueño de otros!
De un rayo húmedo, negro,
vertiendo sangre negra!
Qué corcel espantoso
de brida soñolienta
y látigos de espuma
y patas paralelas!

Aguas del corazón
metidas en el sueño,
olas, canales, lenguas,
en desarrollo lento,
invasoras y activas
trepando al sueño de otros,
escalando silencios,
atravesando párpados,
modificando sueños!

Sueños solos, temibles,
sueños de labios secos,
solos, sin dirección,
en busca de otros sueños,
con boca de vampiros,
en la noche, corriendo,
carcomiendo como ácidos,
saltando sobre sueños,
corroborando espantos,
comunicando muertos.

Campanas de olas muertas,
disparan aves negras
de cartílago inmenso,
alas que agarran sombras,
picos y uñas de sueño,
latitudes golpeadas
de sonidos y vuelos,
sonidos cazadores,
sueños vencidos, húmedos,
respirados, opresos.

NUMBER AND NAME

From one dream to another,
from one dark wet lightning bolt,
shedding black blood.
A horrifying steed
with its sleepy bridle
and whips of spume
and parallel paws.

Waters from the heart
oozing in dreams,
waves, canals, tongues,
in slow evolution,
liquid invaders, clambering
into others' dreams,
changing those dreams
by climbing silences,
across eyelids.

Solitary dreams, fearsome
dry-lipped dreams,
Alone, of no fixed abode,
seeking out fellow dreams
with their vampire mouths,
racing through the night,
rotting like acids,
leaping over dreams,
corroborating terrors,
communicating deaths.

Bells of dead waves
release black birds
with immense cartilages
and wings grasping shadows,
the beaks and nails of dreams,
latitudes whipped
by sounds and flights,
the sounds of hunters,
defeated, dampened dreams
of respiration and oppression.

Sueños que inundan sueños,
crecen y cortan sueños,
tragan y botan sueños,
lavan y tiñen sueños,
hunden y rompen sueños,
sueños que comen sueños,
crecen dentro de sueños,
duermen dentro de sueños,
sueñan dentro de sueños.
Entre barrotes negros,
cerraduras heladas,
escaleras oscuras,
sueño a sueño se amarra,
sueño a sueño se bate,
sueño a sueño baila.
Con espadas de gas,
con estrellas de vino
se sumergen en negros
corredores vacíos,
vagos como cenizas
y largos como ríos,
como ciudades muertas
o ejércitos heridos,
o túneles espesos,
callados y vacíos,
blandos seres que se hunden
o se unen como hilos,
lentas ropas de miedo,
de sopor, de sigilo,
que tiemblan y se caen
como lágrimas de humo,
cenizas instantáneas,
reuniones de olvido.

(La escala vertical
y su paso de plata,
y su cuerpo delgado,
desnudo como el agua,

Dreams that flood other dreams,
swell other dreams, hack down other dreams,
swallow dreams and toss them away again,
wash them and dye them,
sink them and shatter them.
They grow within dreams,
sleep within dreams.
dream within dreams.
Behind black bars
and frozen locks,
down dark stairways,
one dream anchors to another,
one dream fights another,
one dream dances with another.
With gaseous swords
and wine-filled stars,
they dive down empty
black corridors,
as misty as ash
and long as rivers,
like dead cities
or wounded armies,
silent and vacant,
bland beings sinking
or linking arms like threads,
slow trappings of fear,
torpor, stealth,
trembling and tumbling
like tears of smoke,
instant ash,
reunions of forgetting.

(The vertical scale
and its silvery step
and its slender body,
naked as water,

su olor a té y orgullo,
su rostro de topacio,
confusos, titubeando,
corren la noche clara,
tropezando, con sombras,
sedientos como mi alma.)

Domicilios del sueño
con árboles de trapo
y sombras de manzana,
y brillos en el fondo,
brillos heridos, húmedos,
como espadas con sangre
caídas en el agua.

[1933]

SEVERIDAD

Os condeno a cagar de mañana y de noche
leyendo periódicos atrasados y novelas amargas,
os condeno a cagar arrepentimiento y melancolía
y suaves atardeceres amarillos.

Os condeno a cagar en *corset* y en camisa
en vuestras casas llenas de bicicletas y canarios,
con vuestras posaderas azules y alientes
y vuestros lamentables corazones a plazo.

De un mundo hundido salen cosas siniestras:
aparatos mecánicos y perros sin hocico,
embajadores gordos como rosas,
cigarrerías negras y cines averiados.

its scent of tea and pride,
its topaz face,
confused, tottering,
running through the bright night.
hurtling into shadows,
as thirsty as my soul.)

A home for a dream
with ragged trees
and apple-shaped shadows
and a glow at the back,
a damp, damaged glow,
like blood-spattered swords
drowning in water.

SEVERITY

I sentence you to shit from morning to night,
while reading out-of-date newspapers and twisted novels.
I sentence you to shit deep regrets and melancholy
and the sweetest of yellow twilights.

I sentence you to shit into your corsets, on to your shirts,
squatting on your hot blue buttocks
in houses stuffed with bicycles and canaries,
and your lamentable fixed-term hearts.

From your decrepit world, sinister things emerge:
mechanical gadgets and dogs without snouts,
ambassadors as plump as roses,
dingy tobacconists and broken-down cinemas.

Yo os condeno a la noche de los dormitorios
interrumpida apenas por irrigadores y pos sueños,
sueños como eucaliptus de mil hojas
y raíces mojadas en orines y espuma.

No me dejéis tocar vuestras aguas sedentarias
ni vuestras reclamaciones intestinales, ni vuestras religiones,
ni vuestras fotografías prematuramente colgadas:
porque yo tengo llamas en los dedos,
y lágrimas de desventura en el corazón,
y amapolas moribundas anidan en mi boca
como depósitos de sangre infranqueable.

Y odio vuestras abuelas y vuestras moscas,
odio vuestras comidas y vuestros sueños,
y vuestros poetas que escriben sobre «la dulce esposa»,
y «las felicidades de la aldea»:
en verdad merecéis vuestros poetas y vuestros pianos
y vuestros desagradables enredos a cuatro piernas.

Dejadme solo con mi sangre pura,
con mis dedos y mi alma,
y mis sollozos solos, oscuros como túneles.
Dejadme el reino de las largas olas.
Dejadme un buque verde y un espejo.

[1934]

I sentence you to a night in a noisy dormitory,
interrupted by the occasional sprinkler or dream,
dreams like eucalyptus trees with a thousand leaves,
their roots drenched in urine and froth.

Keep me away from your stagnant waters,
your intestinal complaints and your religions,
your photographs hung up far too soon:
because I have flames in my fingers
and tears of misfortune in my heart,
and dying poppies nesting in my mouth
like deposits of impassable blood.

And I hate your grandmothers and your flies,
I hate your meals and your dreams
and your poets who write about 'gentle wives'
and the 'joys of the happy village'.
But in fact, you deserve every one of those poets and pianos
and troublesome four-legged entanglements.

Leave me in peace with my purer blood,
my fingers and my soul,
and my lonely sobs, as dark as tunnels.
Leave me to my kingdom of immense waves.
Leave me to my green boat – and a mirror.

de
EL HONDERO ENTUSIASTA
(1933)

POEMA 5

Amiga, no te mueras.
Óyeme estas palabras que me salen ardiendo,
y que nadie diría si yo no las dijera.

Amiga, no te mueras.

Yo soy el que te espera en la estrellada noche.
El que bajo el sangriento sol poniente te espera.

Miro caer las frutas en la tierra sombría.
Miro bailar las gotas del rocío en las hierbas.

En la noche al espeso perfume de las rosas,
cuando danza la ronda de las sombras inmensas.

Bajo el cielo del sur, el que te espera cuando
el aire de la tarde como una boca besa.

Amiga, no te mueras.

Yo soy el que cortó las guirnaldas rebeldes
para el lecho selvático fragante a sol y a selva.
El que trajo en los brazos jacintos amarillos.
Y rosas desgarradas. Y amapolas sangrientas.

El que cruzó los brazos por esperarte, ahora.
El que quebró sus arcos. El que dobló sus flechas.

Yo soy el que en los labios guarda sabor de uvas.
Racimos refregados. Mordeduras bermejas.

El que te llama desde las llanuras brotadas.
Yo soy el que en la hora del amor te desea.

from
THE ARDENT SLINGSMAN
(1933)

POEM 5

Do not die, my friend.
Listen to these words that I spell out like flames,
words that no one but me will say.

Do not die, my friend.

I am the one waiting for you on this night of stars.
Under the bleeding sun, I am the one who waits.

I watch the fruits dropping on the sombre soil.
I watch the dewdrops dancing in the grass.

At night, the thick perfume of the roses
in the ballet of the giant shadows.

I'm the one who waits under a southern sky,
as the evening air purses its lips in a kiss.

Do not die, my friend.

I am the one who scythed down these rebellious garlands
to make a woodland bed fragrant with sun and forest,
who carried yellow jasmine in his arms.
And roses ripped to shreds. And blood-red poppies.

For you, I've smashed my bows, bent my arrows in two
and lie here now, arms folded, waiting, waiting for you.

I am the one whose lips still taste of grapes
scrubbed clean, lips auburn from all the biting,

calling you from the blossom in the plains,
longing for you in this hour of love.

El aire de la tarde cimbra las ramas altas.
Ebrio, mi corazón, bajo Dios, tambalea.

El río desatado rompe a llorar y a veces
se adelgaza su voz y se hace pura y trémula.

Retumba, atardecida, la queja azul del agua.
Amiga, no te mueras!

Yo soy el que te espera en la estrellada noche,
sobre las playas áureas, sobre las rubias eras.

El que cortó jacintos para tu lecho, y rosas.
¡Tendido entre las hierbas yo soy el que te espera!

The evening air whips the highest branches.
My drunken heart wavers in God's eyes.

Unleashed, the river starts to weep. At times,
its voice dwindles to a quiver of purity.

And when dusk falls, the water echoes with a blue lament.
Do not die, my friend!

I am the one who waits for you on this night of stars,
on golden beaches, on bright threshing floors.

The one who cut down hyacinths for your bed, and roses.
I wait for you, lying ready in the grass.

SÓLO EL HOMBRE

Yo atravesé las hostiles
cordilleras,
entre los árboles pasé a caballo.
El humus ha dejado
en el suelo
su alfombra de mil años.

Los árboles se tocan en la altura,
en la unidad temblorosa.
Abajo, oscura es la selva.
Un vuelo corto, un grito
la atraviesan,
los pájaros del frío,
los zorros de eléctrica cola,
una gran hoja que cae,
y mi caballo pisa el blando
lecho del árbol dormido,
pero bajo la tierra
los árboles de nuevo
se entienden y sé tocan.
La selva es una sola,
un solo gran puñado de perfume,
una sola raíz bajo la tierra.

Las púas me mordían,
las duras piedras herían mi caballo,
él hielo iba buscando bajo mi ropa rota
mi corazón para cantarle y dormirlo.

from
THE GRAPES AND THE WIND
(1954)

ONLY MAN

I crossed hostile cordilleras,
rode my horse between trees.
The ground is carpeted in
a thousand years of peat.

The trees kiss high in the quivering air. Below,
the forest lies in darkness.
A brief flight, a scream,
cold-winged birds,
foxes with electric tails,
a giant leaf tumbling
and my horse trampling
the soft bed of a slumbering tree.
But under the ground
the trees meet again and caress.
The forest is as one,
one great fist of perfume,
a single root beneath the soil.

I was bitten by barbs,
the hard stones wounded my horse,
ice reached beneath my tattered clothes
and sang to my heart before sending it to sleep.

Los ríos que nacían
ante mi vista bajaban veloces
y querían matarme.
De pronto un árbol ocupaba el camino
como si hubiera
echado a andar y entonces
lo hubiera derribado
la selva, y allí estaba
grande como mil hombres,
lleno de cabelleras,
pululado de insectos,
podrido por la lluvia,
pero desde la muerte
quería detenerme.

Yo salté el árbol,
lo rompí con el hacha,
acaricié sus hojas hermosas como manos,
toqué las poderosas
raíces que mucho más que yo
conocían la tierra.
Yo pasé sobre el árbol,
crucé todos los ríos,
la espuma me llevaba,
las piedras me mentían,
el aire verde que creaba
alhajas a cada minuto
atacaba mi frente,
quemaba mis pestañas.
Yo atravesé las altas cordilleras
porque conmigo un hombre,
otro hombre, un hombre
iba conmigo.
No venían los árboles,
no iba conmigo el agua
vertiginosa que quiso matarme,
ni la tierra espinosa.
Sólo el hombre,

I watched rivers being born,
rushing towards me,
trying to kill me.
Suddenly, a tree blocked my path
as if it had walked there
and had been toppled by the forest.
And there it lay
as huge as a thousand men,
all tangled hair,
seething with insects,
rain-rotted,
but still seeking to stop me
in my tracks,
after death.

I leapt over the tree,
broke it up with an axe,
stroked its leaves, as beautiful as hands,
touched the power
of its roots so much more familiar
with the earth than I.
Having leapt the tree,
I crossed every river I met.
The froth carried me in its spray,
the stones whispered their lies to me,
the constant gems of green air
whipped my forehead,
scorched my eyelashes.
I was able to ride the high cordilleras
only because one man,
another man,
rode with me.
Not the trees,
not the dizzying waters
set on murdering me,
nor the thorny earth.
No: only man.

sólo el hombre estaba conmigo.
No las manos del árbol,
hermosas como rostros, ni las graves
raíces que conocen la tierra
me ayudaron.
Sólo el hombre.
No sé cómo se llama.
Era tan pobre como yo, tenía
ojos como los míos, y con ellos
descubría el camino
para que otro hombre pasara.
Y aquí estoy.
Por eso existo.

Creo
que no nos juntaremos en la altura.
Creo
que bajo la tierra nada nos espera,
pero sobre la tierra
vamos juntos.
Nuestra unidad está sobre la tierra.

PALABRAS A EUROPA (FRAGMENTO)

Yo, americano de las tierras pobres,
de las metálicas mesetas,
en donde el golpe del hombre contra el hombre
se agrega al de la tierra sobre el hombre.
Yo, americano errante,
huérfano de los ríos y de los
volcanes que me procrearon,
a vosotros, sencillos europeos
de las calles torcidas,

Only man went with me.
The trees' hands,
finely chiselled as faces,
weren't there for me,
or the soil-loving roots,
when I asked for help.
It was only man.
I don't even know his name.
He was as poor as me,
had eyes like mine, and those eyes
lit up the path ahead
for other men to follow.
And here I am.
That's why I exist.

I don't believe we'll meet in Heaven
nor that anything awaits us below ground.
But on earth,
we'll ride together,
on earth we'll be as one.

WORDS FOR EUROPE (EXTRACT)

I am an American from the poor lands,
from the metallic *meseta*,
where man beats man
as the soil beats man.
I'm a wandering American,
an orphan of the rivers and the
volcanoes that procreated me.
To you, simple Europeans
in your twisted streets,

humildes propietarios de la paz y el aceite,
sabios tranquilos como el humo,
yo os digo: aquí he venido
a aprender de vosotros,
de unos y otros, de todos,
porque de qué me serviría
la tierra, para qué se hicieron
el mar y los caminos,
sino para ir mirando y aprendiendo
de todos los seres un poco.
No me cerréis la puerta
(como las puertas negras, salpicadas de sangre
de mi materna España).
No me mostréis la guadaña enemiga
ni el escuadrón blindado,
ni las antiguas horcas para el nuevo ateniense,
en las anchas vías gastadas
por el resplandor de las uvas.
No quiero ver un soldadito muerto
con los ojos comidos.
Mostradme de una patria a otra
el infinito hilo de la vida
cosiendo el traje de la primavera.

CABELLERA DE CAPRI

Capri, reina de rocas,
en tu vestido
de color amaranto y azucena
viví desarrollando
la dicha y el dolor, la viña llena
de radiantes racimos
que conquisté en la tierra,

humble growers of oil and peace,
with a wisdom as calm as smoke,
I say just this: I came here
to learn from you,
from one and all of you,
Because what good is the soil,
the sea and the roads
if you can't look and learn
from everyone?
Don't slam the door on me
(like the black, blood-spattered doors
of Mother Spain).
Don't show me an enemy scythe
or an armoured squadron
or the old gallows for the new Athenians.
I don't want to see another dead soldier
with his eyes eaten away
lying in a wide streets eroded
by the radiance of grapes.
Show me the infinite life-thread
from one land to another,
the suit of spring...

TANGLE OF CAPRI HAIR

Capri, you are my rocky queen.
In the folds of your skirts
of crimson amaranths and lilies,
I lived through happiness and pain.
I conquered your vineyards
and the joys of earthbound clusters,

el trémulo tesoro
de aroma y cabellera,
lámpara cenital, rosa extendida,
panal de mi planeta.
Desembarqué en invierno.
Su traje de zafiro
la isla en sus pies guardaba,
y desnuda surgía en su vapor
de catedral marina.
Era de piedra su hermosura. En cada
fragmento de su piel reverdecía
la primavera pura
que escondía en las grietas su tesoro.
Un relámpago rojo y amarillo
bajo la luz delgada
yacía soñoliento
esperando la hora
de desencadenar su poderío.
En la orilla de pájaros inmóviles,
en mitad de del cielo,
un ronco grito, el viento
y la indecible espuma.
De plata y piedra tu vestido, apenas
la flor azul estalla
bordando el manto hirsuto
con su sangre celeste.
Oh soledad de Capri, vino
de las uvas de plata,
copa de invierno, plena
de ejercicio invisible,
levanté tu firmeza,
tu delicada luz, tus estructuras,
y tu alcohol de estrella
bebí como si fuera
naciendo en mí la vida.
Isla, de tus paredes
desprendí la pequeña flor nocturna
y la guardo en mi pecho.

the tremulous treasures
of perfume and tangled hair:
a light above me, a rose around me,
my honeycomb planet.
I landed in winter.
The island's sapphire suit
lay at its feet and, naked,
it stood to greet me, vaporous
as a cathedral in the sea.
It had a beauty all of stone
but every pore of its skin came back
to life with the purity of spring,
and every niche revealed a hidden jewel.
A drowsy bolt of lightning dozed
behind flimsy curtains of light,
its reds and yellows
ready to unleash their might.
A raucous shriek from birds
hovering in the sky
pierced the wind and the
untold secrets of sea-spray.
Your clothes are woven
from silver and from stone
and when a blue flower explodes,
it braids your cloak of bristles
in celestial blood.
Oh, the solitude of Capri,
wine born from silvery grapes,
a glass filled to the brim
with unseen energy,
I drank to the delicacy
of your light, to your every form,
to your star-lit alcohol,
drank as if life itself were
welling up inside me.
My island, from your walls
I picked a tiny flower of night
and held it against my chest.

Y desde el mar girando en tu contorno
hice un anillo de agua
que allí quedó en las olas,
encerrando las torres orgullosas
de piedra florecida,
las cumbres agrietadas
que mi amor sostuvieron
y guardarán con manos implacables
la huella de mis besos.

LA POLICÍA

Nosotros somos
de la policía.
– Y usted? Quién es?
De dónde viene, a dónde
pretende dirigirse?
Su padre? Su cuñado?
Con quién durmió las siete noches últimas?
– Yo dormí con mi amor, yo soy tal vez,
tal vez, tal vez,
soy de la Poesía.

Y así una góndola
más negra que las otras
detrás de mí los transportó en Venecia,
en Bologna en la noche,
en el tren: soy una sombra errante
seguida por las sombras.
Yo vi en Venecia, erguido el Campanile
elevando entre las palomas de San Marcos
su tricornio de policía.

Out at sea, I wrote your name
in a ring of water
around your proud towers
of blossoming stone,
around those creviced heights
that sustained my love
and hold the trace of my kisses
in your unyielding hands.

THE POLICE

We're from
the police.
And who are you?
Where do you come from?
Where are you planning to go?
Who's your father? Your brother-in law?
Who did you sleep with over the past seven days?
'I slept with my love and perhaps,
perhaps, just perhaps,
I come from Poetry.'

And then a gondola,
blacker than the others,
came up behind me and headed
to Venice, or by train to Bologna,
in the night: I'm a wandering shadow
hunted down by other shadows.
I saw their three-cornered hats
in Venice, at the top of the Campanile,
soaring among the pigeons in St Mark's Square.

Y Paulina, desnuda, en el museo,
cuando besé su bella boca fría
me dijo: Tiene en orden sus papeles?
En la casa de Dante
bajo los viejos techos florentinos
hay interrogatorios, y David
con sus ojos de mármol, sin pupilas
se olvidó de su padre, Buonarroti,
porque lo obligan cada día a contar
lo que con ojos ciegos ha mirado.
Sin embargo aquel día
en que me trasladaban a la frontera suiza
la policía se encontró de pronto
que la salía al paso
la militante poesía.
No olvidaré la multitud romana
que en la estación, de noche,
me sacó de las manos
de la perseguidora policía.

Cómo olvidar el gesto guerrillero
de Guttuso y el rostro de Guiliano,
la ola de ira, el golpe en las narices
de los sabuesos, cómo olvidar a Mario,
de quien en el exilio
aprendí a amar la libertad de Italia,
y ahora iracunda su cabeza blanca
divisé confundiéndose
en el mar agitado
de mis amigos y de mis enemigos?
No olvidaré el pequeño
paraguas de Elsa Morante
cayendo sobre un pecho policial
como el pesado pétalo
de una fuerza florida.

Y así en Italia
por voluntad del pueblo,

And when I kissed Paulina,
on her beautiful cold mouth,
as she lay there, naked, in the museum,
she said: 'Are your papers in order?'
They conduct their interrogations
in Dante's house
under old Florentine roofs,
and David, with his empty eyes of marble,
forgot about his father, Michelangelo,
because he was duty-bound
to file a daily report about
what he'd seen, despite his blindness.
And yet on that day,
as they transferred me to the Swiss border,
the police suddenly found themselves
waylaid by militant ranks of poetry.
I'll never forget the crowds in Rome:
at night, in that station,
they freed me from the hands
of my police pursuers.

How could I forget Guttuso
and his warrior gestures, Giuliano's face,
the wave of fury, the blows to the nostrils
of the bloodhounds? How could I forget
Mario, who taught me to love Italy's freedom
while I was in exile?
I spotted his angry white hair
bobbing up and down in the turbulent sea
of all my friends and enemies.
I will never forget Elsa Morante's tiny umbrella
striking a policeman's chest
like a heavy petal but
with the force of a flower.

And so, in Italy,
with the people's wishes,

peso de poesía,
firmeza solidaria,
acción de la ternura
se quedó mi destino.
Y así fue cómo
fue este libro naciendo
rodeado de mar y limoneros,
escuchando en silencio,
detrás del muro de la policía,
cómo luchaba y lucha,
cómo cantaba y canta
el valeroso pueblo
que ganó una batalla para que yo pudiera
descansar en la isla que me esperaba
con una rama en flor de jasmín en su boca
y en sus pequeñas manos la fuente de mi canto.

LA PASAJERA DE CAPRI

De dónde, planta o rayo,
de dónde, rayo negro o planta dura,
venías y viniste
hasta el rincón marino?

Sombra del continente más lejano
hay en tus ojos, luna abierta
en tu boca salvaje,
y tu rostro es el párpado de una fruta dormida.
El pezón satinado de una estrella es tu forma,
sangre y fuego de antiguas lanzas hay en tus labios.

De dónde recogiste
pétalos transparentes

and the sheer weight of poetry,
the strength of solidarity
and so many tender gestures,
my fate was decided.
That was how this book
took shape: surrounded
by sea and lemon trees,
I listened in silence
behind police walls,
to the courage of the people,
struggling, then as now,
singing, then as now,
winning the battle so I could find
peace on an island waiting for me
with a bouquet of jasmine between its lips
and the source of my song in its hands.

PASSENGER IN CAPRI

Where did you come from?
From which plant, which flash of lightning,
black bolt or stiffened flower
did you come to this corner of the sea?

There's a shadow of the most distant continent
in your eyes, an open moon
in your savage mouth,
and your face is the eyelid of a slumbering fruit.
You're shaped like the satin nipple of a star
and your lips blaze with the blood and fire of ancient lances.

Where did you pick those
transparent petals

de manantial, de dónde
trajiste la semilla
que reconozco? Y luego
el mar de Capri en ti, mar extranjero,
detrás de ti las rocas, el aceite,
la recta claridad bien construida,
pero tú, yo conozco,
yo conozco esa rosa,
yo conozco la sangre de esa rosa,
yo sé que la conozco
yo sé de dónde viene,
y huelo el aire libre de ríos y caballos
que tu presencia trae a mi memoria.
Tu cabellera es una carta roja
llena de bruscos besos y noticias,
tu afirmación, tu investidura clara
me hablan a mediodía,
a medianoche llaman a mi puerta
como si adivinaran
adónde quieren regresar mis pasos.

Tal vez, desconocida,
la sal de Maracaibo
suena en tu voz llenándola de sueño,
o el frío viento de Valparaíso
sacudió tu razón cuando crecías.
Lo cierto es que hoy, mirándote al pasar
entre las aves de pecho rosado
de los farallones de Capri,
la llamarada de tus ojos, algo
que vi volar desde tu pecho, el aire
que rodea tu piel, la luz nocturna
que de tu corazón sin duda sale,
algo llegó a mi boca
con un sabor de flor que conocía,
algo tiñó mis labios con el licor oscuro
de las plantas silvestres de mi infancia,
y yo pensé: Esta dama,

of spring water, where
did you find that seed
I know so well? And
you hold the sea of Capri within you, a foreign sea.
Behind you, the rocks, olive oil,
the honest, well-constructed clarity.
But you – I know you,
I know that rose,
I recognise the blood of that rose,
I'm sure I know it,
know where it comes from.
And I remember the unsoiled air of rivers and horses:
your presence carries those echoes to me.
Your tangled hair is the red scrawl of a letter
bearing sudden kisses and good news.
Your appointment was confirmed
in words in the gleam of midday,
and at midnight they knock on my door
as if they knew full well
that I wanted to stroll back into the past.

And yet you're still a stranger, perhaps.
The salt of Maracaibo
rings out in your voice with the fullness of sleep.
When you were young, the chill wind of Valparaíso
shook your reason to the core.
The truth is, watching you today,
walking among the pink-chested birds
on Capri's headlands,
with a flare in your eyes, or whatever it was
that flew from your breast, the air
that floats above your skin, the nocturnal light
beaming from your heart,
something reached my mouth
with the taste of a familiar flower,
something stained my lips with the black liquor
of those wild plants of my childhood
and I thought: who is this lady?

aunque el clásico azul derrame todos
los racimos del cielo en su garganta,
aunque detrás de ella los templos
nimben con su blancura coronada
tanta hermosura,
ella no es, ella es otra,
algo crepita en ella que me llama:
toda la tierra que me dio la vida
está en esta mirada, y estas manos
sutiles
recogieron el agua en la vertiente
y estos menudos pies fueron midiendo
las volcánicas islas de mi patria.

Oh tú, desconocida, dulce y dura,
cuando ya tu paso
descendió hasta perderse,
y sólo las columnas
del templo roto y el zafiro verde
del mar que canta en mi destierro
quedaron solos, solos
conmigo y con tu sombra,
mi corazón dio un gran latido,
como si una gran piedra sostenida
en la invisible altura
cayera de repente
sobre el agua y saltaran las espumas.

Y desperté de tu presencia entonces
con el rostro regado
por tu salpicadura
agua y aroma y sueño,
distancia y tierra y ola!

even if the ancient blue
of sky and grapes fills her throat;
even if the white crowns
of the temples behind her
cloud her beauty,
it's not her, it's another lady
Something in her blazes, beckons to me:
the land that gave birth to me, all of it,
lies in her glance, those soft hands
gathered water on the slopes
and those tiny feet paced
the volcanic islands of my homeland.

Oh, sweet, hardened stranger,
when your footprints
faded and the pillars
of shattered temples and green sapphire
of the sea were abandoned, all alone,
alone with me and with your shadow,
my heart pounded
as if a huge boulder hanging
in the invisible heights
had suddenly toppled
into the water with an explosion of spray.

And I awoke from your presence
with my face covered
in your splashing,
water and aroma and dreams,
distance and land and waves.

CUÁNDO DE CHILE?

Oh Chile, largo pétalo
de mar y vino y nieve,
ay cuándo
ay cuándo y cuándo
ay cuándo
me encontraré contigo,
enrollarás tu cinta
de espuma blanca y negra en mi cintura,
desencadenaré mi poesía
sobre tu territorio.

Hay hombres
mitad pez, mitad viento,
hay otros hombres hechos de agua.
Yo estoy hecho de tierra.
Voy por el mundo
cada vez más alegre:
cada ciudad me da una nueva vida.
El mundo está naciendo.
Pero si llueve en Lota
sobre mí cae la lluvia,
si en Lonquimay la nieve
resbala de las hojas
llega la nieve donde estoy.
Crece en mí el trigo oscuro de Cautín.
Yo tengo una araucaria en Villarrica,
tengo arena en el Norte Grande,
tengo una rosa rubia en la provincia,
y el viento que derriba
la última ola de Valparaíso
me golpea en el pecho
con un ruido quebrado
como si allí tuviera
mi corazón una ventana rota.

WHEN, CHILE?

Oh Chile, long petal
of sea and wine and snow,
when
and when and when,
when will I see you again?
When will you wrap your ribbon
of black and white foam around my waist
and when will I unfold my poetry
all over you?

There are men
who are half fish, half wind.
Others are made of water.
I'm made of soil.
I travel the world
happier than ever:
Each city brings me back to life.
The world is being reborn.
But if it rains in Lota,
the rain falls on me;
if in Lonquimay, the snow
slides off the leaves,
that snow reaches me too.
The dark wheat of Cautín grows within me.
I have a monkey-puzzle tree in Villarica,
and in the Norte Grande,
a fair-skinned rose in the provinces,
and the wind that topples
the very last wave in Valparaíso
whips my chest
with a faltering thud
as if shattering a glass window
in my heart.

El mes de octubre ha llegado hace
tan poco tiempo del pasado octubre
que cuando éste llegó fue como si
me estuviera mirando el tiempo inmóvil.
Aquí es otoño. Cruzo
la estepa siberiana.
Día tras día todo es amarillo,
el árbol y la usina,
la tierra y lo que en ella el hombre nuevo crea:
hay oro y llama roja,
mañana inmensidad, nieve, pureza.

En mi país la primavera
viene de norte a sur con su fragancia.
Es como una muchacha
que por las piedras negras de Coquimbo,
por la orilla solemne de la espuma
vuela con pies desnudos
hasta los archipiélagos heridos.
No sólo territorio, primavera,
llenándome, me ofreces.
No soy un hombre solo.
Nací en el sur. De la frontera
traje las soledades y el galope
del último caudillo.
Pero el Partido me bajó del caballo
y me hice hombre, y anduve
los arenales y las cordilleras
amando y descubriendo.

Pueblo mío, verdad que en primavera
suena mi nombre en tus oídos
y tú me reconoces
como si fuera un río
que pasa por tu puerta?

Soy un río. Si escuchas
pausadamente bajo los salares

October arrives so soon
after the last that it seems
as though time has stopped still.
It's autumn here. I'm crossing
the Siberian steppes.
Every day is a yellow day,
everything is yellow:
trees and factories,
the soil and everything man grows in it –
gold and red flames,
an immense morning, snow, purity.

In my country, the fragrance of spring
arrives from north to south
like a barefooted girl
flying over the black stones of Coquimbo,
over the solemn banks of spume,
to the wounded archipelagos.
You offer me land and
fill me with spring.
I'm not a lonely man.
I was born in the south. From the frontier,
I brought solitude and the gallop
of the final caudillo.
But the Party dragged me off my horse
and made me a man, and I wandered
over the sands and the cordilleras,
loving and discovering.

Is it really true that my name
rings out in my country's ears
and you recognise it
like a river flowing
through your doors?

I am a river. If you pause
to listen beneath the salt flats

de Antofagasta, o bien
al sur, de Osorno
o hacia la cordillera, en Melipilla,
o en Temuco, en la noche
de astros mojados y laurel sonoro,
pones sobre la tierra tus oídos,
escucharás que corro
sumergido, cantando.

Octubre, oh primavera,
devuélveme a mi pueblo.
Qué haré sin ver mil hombres,
mil muchachas,
qué haré sin conducir sobre mis hombros
una parte de la esperanza?
Qué haré sin caminar con la bandera
que de mano en mano en la fila
de nuestra larga lucha
llegó a las manos mías?
Ay Patria, Patria,
ay Patria, cuándo
ay cuándo y cuándo
cuándo
me encontraré contigo?

Lejos de ti
mitad de tierra tuya y hombre tuyo
he continuado siendo,
y otra vez hoy la primavera pasa.
Pero yo con tus flores me he llenado,
con tu victoria voy sobre la frente
y en ti siguen viviendo mis raíces.

Ay cuándo
encontraré tu primavera dura,
y entre todos tus hijos
andaré por tus campos y tus calles
con mis zapatos viejos.

of Antofagasta, or
south of Osorno,
or towards the cordillera, in Melapilla
in Temuco, on a night
of wet stars and sweet-sounding laurel,
put your ear to the ground
and you will hear me
running and singing there.

It's October. Take me home
to the spring in my country.
How can I cope without the sight
of a thousand men, a thousand girls?
Without carrying on my shoulders
at least part of all your hopes?
Without walking in line until the flag
passing from hand to hand
in our long struggle,
reaches mine?

Oh my homeland, my homeland.
When,
when and when,
when will I see you again?

I'm so far from you,
Yet always half of me feels your soil
beneath me, half of me is you.
The spring has vanished yet again.
but I'm full of your blossom
your roots still live within me.
my forehead bears the wrinkles of your victory.

When will I see your harsh spring,
walk with your children
through the fields and streets
in my time-worn shoes?

Ay cuándo
iré con Elías Lafferte
por toda la pampa dorada.
Ay cuándo a ti te apretaré la boca,
chilena que me esperas,
con mis labios errantes?
Ay cuándo
podré entrar en la sala del Partido
a sentarme con Pedro Fogonero,
con el que no conozco y sin embargo
es más hermano mío que mi hermano.
Ay cuándo
me sacará del sueño un trueno verde
de tu manto marino.
Ay cuándo, Patria, en las elecciones
iré de casa en casa recogiendo
la libertad temerosa
para que grite en medio de la calle.
Ay cuándo, Patria,
te casarás conmigo
con ojos verdemar y vestido de nieve
y tendremos millones de hijos nuevos
que entregarán la tierra a los hambrientos.

Ay Patria, sin harapos,
ay primavera mía,
ay cuándo
ay cuándo y cuándo
despertaré en tus brazos
empapado de mar y de rocío.
Ay cuando yo esté cerca
de ti, te tomaré de la cintura,
nadie podrá tocarte,
yo podré defenderte
cantando,
cuando
vaya contigo, cuando
vayas conmigo, cuándo
ay cuándo.

When will I cross
the golden pampas
with Elías Lafferte?
When will I lock my wandering lips
on to yours, my Chilean one?
When will I
sit down with Pedro Fogonero
at Party headquarters –
I don't even know him and yet
he's more of a brother to me than my own.

When will my dreams of green thunder
rolling over cloaks of sea come true again?
When will I go from door to door,
at election time, collecting
fearful freedoms to be
declared out loud in the street?
When, my homeland
with your sea-green eyes,
will you marry me
in your wedding dress of snow
so we can have millions of children
to hand out land to the hungry?

Homeland, dressed not in rags but in your finery
at springtime,
when
and when and when
will I wake up in your arms,
sweating in sea and dew?
When I'm near you again,
I'll take you by the waist,
and no one else will touch you.
I'll protect you
with my song
when I'm with you,
when you're with me.
When,
oh when?

UN DÍA

A ti, amor, este día
a ti te lo consagro.
Nació azul, con un ala
blanca en mitad del cielo.
Llegó la luz
a la inmovilidad de los cipreses.
Los seres diminutos
salieron a la orilla de una hoja
o a la mancha del sol en una piedra.
Y el día sigue azul
hasta que entre en la noche como un río
y haga temblar la sombra con sus aguas azules.
A ti, amor, este día.

Apenas, desde lejos, desde el sueño,
lo presentí y apenas
me tocó su tejido
de red incalculable
yo pensé: es para ella.
Fue un latido de plata,
fue sobre el mar volando un pez azul,
fue un contacto de arenas deslumbrantes,
fue el vuelo de una flecha
que entre el cielo y la tierra
atravesó mi sangre
y como un rayo recogí en mi cuerpo
la desbordada claridad del día.

Es para ti, amor mío.

Yo dije: es para ella.
Este vestido es suyo.
El relámpago azul que se detuvo
sobre el agua y la tierra
a ti te lo consagro.

A ti, amor, este día.

THIS DAY

My love, I dedicate
this day to you.
It was born blue, with one
white wing in the sky.
The light kissed
still cypresses.
Tiny creatures
crept towards the rim of a leaf
or towards the stain of the sun on a stone.
And the day clings to its blue
until it penetrates night like a river
and the shadows shiver in watery azure.
To you, my love, this day.

As soon as I felt it open up,
from afar, from my sleep,
felt it touch me with its
priceless tissue of nets,
I thought: it's for her.
It was a silver heartbeat,
it was a blue fish flying over the sea,
it was the warmth of dazzling sand,
the flight of an arrow
from the sky to the earth
piercing my veins,
a bolt of lightning within me
brimming over with the glow of the day.

It's for you, my love.

I said: it's for her.
This dress is hers.
To you I dedicate
the blue lightning that hovers
over land and sea.

To you, my love, this day.

Como una copa eléctrica
o una corola de agua temblorosa,
levántalo en tus manos,
bébelo con los ojos y la boca,
derrámalo en tus venas para que arda
la misma luz en tu sangre y la mía.

Y te doy este día
con todo lo que traiga:
las transparentes uvas de zafiro
y la ráfaga rota
que acerque a tu ventana
los dolores del mundo.

Yo te doy todo el día.
De claridad y de dolor haremos
el pan de nuestra vida,
sin rechazar lo que nos traiga el viento
ni recoger sólo la luz del cielo,
sino las cifras ásperas
de la sombra en la tierra.

Todo te pertenece.
Todo este día con su azul racimo
y la secreta lágrima de sangre
que tú encontrarás en la tierra

Y no te cegará la oscuridad
ni la luz deslumbrante:
de este amasijo humano
están hechas las vidas
y de este pan del hombre comeremos.

Y nuestro amor hecho de luz oscura
y de sombra radiante
será como este día vencedor
que entrará como un río
de claridad en medio de la noche.

Take it in your hands,
electric like a wineglass
or a trembling petal of water,
Drink it in with your eyes and your mouth,
pour it into your veins so that the same light
blazes in your blood and mine.

I give you this day
and all that comes with it:
the translucent grapes of sapphire
and the strangled gust of wind
that brings the sorrows of the world
up to your window.

I give you the whole day.
We'll feed off joy and pain
every day: never rebuff
what the wind carries in, embrace
both the light in the sky
and the rugged shapes
of shadows here on earth.

It all belongs to you,
this day, with its clusters of blue
and the secret teardrop of blood
waiting for you in the ground.

You won't be blinded by the dark
or the ravishing light:
life is made from human tangles,
let's gorge ourselves on human bread.

And our love, born of dark glitters
and radiant shade,
will be like this day,
like a river invading the night
in a victory of brilliance.

Toma este día, amada.
Todo este día es tuyo.

Se lo doy a tus ojos, amor mío,
se lo doy a tu pecho,
te lo dejo en las manos y en el pelo,
como un ramo celeste.
Te lo doy para que hagas un vestido
de plata azul y de agua.
Cuando llegue
la noche que este día inundará
con su red temblorosa,
tiéndete junto a mí,
con todos los tejidos estrellados
de la luz y la sombra
y cierra tus ojos entonces
para que yo me duerma.

LONDRES

En la alta noche, Londres,
apenas entrevista,
ojos innumerables,
dura secreta sombra,
tiendas llenas de sillas,
sillas y sillas, sillas.
El cielo negro
sentado sobre Londres,
sobre su niebla negra,
zapatos y zapatos,
río y río,
calles desmoronadas por los dientes
de la miseria color de hierro,

Take this day, my darling.
The whole day is yours.

I give it to your eyes, my love,
I give it to your breasts,
I leave it in your hands, in your hair,
like a celestial bouquet.
I give it to you to make a dress
from silvery blue and water.
And when night drowns day
in its quivering net,
lie down with me,
touch me and cover me
with all the starry tissue
of light and dark.
And then close your eyes
so I can sleep.

LONDON

It's the middle of the night,
London, you're a mere glimmer,
so many eyes,
a dark, harsh secret,
shopfronts stuffed with chairs,
chairs and more chairs,
the black sky
sitting on London,
on its black fog,
shoes and more shoes,
the river and more river,
streets gnawed by the teeth
of iron-hued squalor

y bajo la basura
el poeta Eliot
con su viejo frac
leyendo a los gusanos.
Me preguntaron cuándo
nací, por qué venía
a perturbar el Imperio.
Todo era policía
con libros y matracas.
Me preguntaron
por mi abuelo y mis tíos,
por mis personalísimos asuntos.
Eran fríos
los jóvenes cuchillos
sobre los cuales
se sienta
sienta
sienta
la matrona Inglaterra,
siempre sentada
sobre millones de desgarraduras,
sobre pobres naciones andrajosas,
sentada
sobre su océano
de reservado uso personal.
océano
de sudor, sangre y lágrimas
de otros pueblos.
Allí sentada
con sus viejos encajes
tomando té y oyendo
los mismos cuentos tontos
de princesas,
coronaciones
y duques conyugales.
Todo pasa entre hadas.
Mientras tanto
ronda la muerte con sombrero
victoriano

and beneath the garbage,
the poet Eliot
in his shabby tail-coat
reading to the worms.
They asked me when I was born,
what I was doing here
disturbing the Empire.
Police everywhere
with their books and rattles.
They interrogated me
about my grandparents and my uncles,
about my most intimate personal affairs.
I felt the cold,
youthful knives
cushioning,
cushioning England,
matron,
midwife England,
sitting on millions of tears,
on poor tattered nations,
sitting in the sea,
its own private sea
of sweat, blood and tears
shed by other nations.
Sitting there
in her ancient lace,
drinking tea and listening
to the same stupid stories
of princesses,
coronations
and the marriages of dukes.
One fairy tale after another. And all the while,
death loiters in its
Victorian hat

y esqueleto raído
por las ennegrecidas gusaneras
de los negros suburbios.
Mientras tanto
la policía te interroga:
es la palabra paz la que les clava
como una bayoneta. Esta palabra paz
ellos quisieran
enterrarla,
pero
no pueden por ahora.
Le echan encima sombra,
niebla
de policía,
la amarran y la encierran,
la golpean,
la salpican de sangre y martirio,
la interrogan,
la echan al mar profundo
con una piedra en cada
sílaba,
la queman con un hierro,
con un sable
la cortaban,
le echan vinagre, hiel, mentira,
la empaquetan,
la llenan de ceniza,
la despeñan.
Pero entonces
vuela
de nuevo
la paloma:
es la palabra paz con plumas nuevas,
es el jazmín del mundo
que avanza con sus pétalos,
es la estrella de sueño y del trabajo,
el ave blanca

and a skeleton gnawed
by blackened maggots
in blackened suburbs.
Meanwhile,
the police keep on questioning:
it's that word 'peace' that nails them
like a bayonet.
They'd love to bury
that word peace
but they can't –
not for now.
They throw everything at it:
shadows,
a thick fog
of policemen,
they handcuff it and
lock it away,
give it a thrashing,
spatter it with blood and martyrdom,
interrogate it,
toss it deep into the sea
with a stone attached
to every syllable,
brand it with a hot-iron,
rip it to shreds
with a sable,
drench it in vinegar, ice, lies,
bundle it up,
stuff it with ashes
and throw it off a cliff.
But then
the dove takes flight
again:
the peace word with new feathers,
the world's jasmine
spreading its petals,
a star of dreams, of work,
the white bird

de vuelo inmaculado,
la rosa que navega,
el pan de todas las vidas,
la estrella de todos los hombres.

LLEGADA A PUERTO PICASSO

Desembarqué en Picasso a las seis de los días de otoño, recién
el cielo anunciaba su desarrollo rosa, miré alrededor, Picasso
se extendía y encendía como el fuego del amanecer. Lejos atrás
quedaban las cordilleras azules y entre ellas levantándose en el
    valle el Arlequín de ceniza.
He aquí: yo venía de Antofagasta y de Maracaibo, yo venía de
    Tucumán
y de la tercera Patagonia, aquella de dientes helados roídos por el
    trueno, aquella de bandera sumergida en la nieve perpetua.

Y yo entonces desembarqué, y vi grandes mujeres de color de
    manzana
en las orillas de Picasso, ojos desmedidos, brazos que reconocí:
tal vez la Amazonia, tal vez era la Forma.

Y al oeste eran titiriteros desvalidos rodando hacia el amarillo,
y músicos con todos los cuadros de la música, y aún más, allá la
    geografía
se pobló de una desgarradora emigración de mujeres, de aristas,
de pétalos y llamas,
y en medio de Picasso entre las dos llanuras y el árbol de vidrio,
vi una Guernica en que permaneció la sangre como un gran río,
    cuya corriente
se convirtió en la copa del caballo y la lámpara:

in immaculate flight,
a navigating rose,
the bread of all our lives,
the star of all men.

ARRIVING AT PORT PICASSO

I came ashore at six o'clock on an autumn morning
with the sky already screaming pink. I looked around.
There it was: Port Picasso, spread out and
blazing with the flames of dawn.
I'd left the blue cordilleras far behind me
and the Harlequin of ash rising from the valleys.
The thing is this: I was arriving from Antofagasta,
from Maracaibo, from Tucumán,
from Patagonia, the third Patagonia
with its ice-cold teeth corroded by thunder
and a flag buried in perpetual snow.

And so, when I disembarked, I saw tall, apple-coloured women
on coastline of Port Picasso, with enormous eyes
and arms I seemed to recognise:
shaped like Amazonians, perhaps; or maybe Form itself.

To the west, I watched hapless puppeteers
heading towards dashes of yellow,
and musicians with their canvases of melody
and, further off, all of geography framed
by heartrending scenes of women departing, petals, flames,
and in the very heart of Port Picasso,
between the two plains and a tree of glass,
I picked out a Guernica, bleeding with the free-flowing blood
of an immense river, a constant current
converted into a wine glass, a horse, a lamp:

ardiente sangre sube a los hocicos,
húmeda luz que acusa para siempre.

Así, pues, en las tierras de Picasso de Sur a Oeste,
toda la vida y las vidas hacían de morada
y el mar y el mundo allí fueron acumulando
su cereal y su salpicadura.

Encontré allí el arañado fragmento
de la tiza, la cáscara del cobre,
y la herradura muerta que desde sus heridas
hacia la eternidad de los metales crece,
y vi la tierra entrar como el pan en los hornos
y la vi aparecer con un hijo sagrado.

También el gallo negro de encefálica espuma
encontré, con un ramo de alambre y arrabales,
el gato azul con su abanico de uñas,
el tigre adelantado sobre los esqueletos.

Yo fui reconociendo las marcas que temblaron
en la desembocadura del agua en que nací.
Primero fue esta piedra con espinas, en donde
sobresalió, ilusoria, la rama desgarrada,
y la madera en cuya rota genealogía
nacen las bruscas aves de mi fuego natal.

Pero el toro asomó desde los corredores
en el centro terrestre, yo vi su voz, llegaba
escarbando las tierras de Picasso, se cubría
la efigie con los mantos de la tinta violeta,
y vi venir el cuello de su oscura catástrofe
y todos los bordados de su baba invencible.

Picasso de Altamira, Toro del Orinoco,
torre de aguas por el amor endurecidas,
tierra de minerales manos que convirtieron
como el arado, en parto la inocencia del musgo.

scorching blood, searing through snouts,
a damp light, forever accusing.

And so, in these Picasso lands, from south to west.
every life, all life, was a dwelling
and the sea and the world accumulated
cereals and splashy consequences.

I found a notched fragment
of chalk, a husk of copper
and a horseshoe, dead from its wounds
but billowing in an eternity of metal.
And I saw the land sliding towards me slowly, like bread
    slipping into an oven
only to emerge again, with its sacred offspring.

I came across the black rooster of encephalic froth,
garlanded with a bouquet of barbed wire from the slums,
the blue cat with its fanned fingernails,
the tiger advancing on skeletons.

I began to make out scars trembling
in the watery mouth where I was born.
First, there was the thorn-covered stone,
and jutting from it, the tattered illusion of a wooden branch,
the shattered lineage of sudden birds from my native fire.

Yet there was the bull, peering out from the central strips
of land. I could see it roaring as it approached,
scratching around in the soil of Port Picasso,
an effigy cloaked in blankets of violet ink.
I saw its neck of dark catastrophe
and the embroidery of invincible spittle.

Picasso from Altamira, Bull from the Orinoco,
a tower of love-hardened water,
a territory of mineral hands that, like a plough,
turned innocent clumps of moss into child-bearers.

Aquí está el toro de cuya cola arrastra
la sal y la aspereza, y en su ruedo
tiembla el collar de España con un sonido seco,
como un saco de huesos que la luna derrama.

Oh circo en que la seda sigue ardiendo
como un olvido de amapolas en la arena
y ya no hay sino día, tiempo, tierra, destino
para enfrentarse, toro del aire desbocado.
Esta corrida tiene todo el morado luto,
la bandera del vino que rompió las vasijas:
y aún más: es la planta de polvo del arriero
y las acumuladas vestiduras que guardan
el distante silencio de la carnicería.
Sube España por estas escaleras, arrugas
de oro y de hambre, y el rostro cerrado de la cólera
y aún más, examinad su abanico: no hay párpados.
Hay una negra luz que nos mira sin ojos.

Padre de la Paloma, que con ella
desplegada en la luz llegaste al día,
recién fundada en su papel de rosa,
recién limpia de sangre y de rocío,
a la clara reunión de las banderas.

Paz o paloma, apostura radiante!

Círculo, reunión de lo terrestre!

Espiga pura entre las flechas rojas!
Súbita dirección de la esperanza!
Contigo estamos en el fondo revuelto
de la arcilla, y hoy en el duradero
metal de la esperanza.

"Es Picasso",
dice la pescadora, atando plata,
y el nuevo otoño araña el estandarte

Here it comes, the bull with a tail sweeping away
all salt and sourness. The necklace of Spain
quivers with a dry thud
like a sack of bones scattered by the moon.

It's a circus of silk, still flaring
like poppies forgotten in the sand.
And all that's left is day, time, land, fate:
they face one other, face the bull, too, in the unbridled air.
This bullfight is all set: for purple mourning,
for the banner of wine bursting from vessels.
And still more: for the dusty plant of the muleteer
and the layers of clothes guarding
the distant silence of carnage.
Spain climbs these steps, these wrinkles
of gold and hunger, its face clenched in anger.
And still more: take a look at the Spanish fan –
it has no eyelids, no eyes, just a dark light
staring blankly back at us.

Father of the Dove, spread out in the daylight,
you arrived in the morning, new-born on pink paper,
freshly cleansed of blood and dew,
for a dazzling reunion of flags.

Peace or dove, what radiant elegance!

A circle, a terrestrial reunion!

A pure sprig of wheat among the red arrows!
A sudden address for all our hopes!
We're with you, today, standing in a pit
of tousled clay and durable,
steel-rimmed optimism.

It's Picasso,'
says the fisherwoman, tying up her silverware,
and another autumn scrapes against

del pastor: el cordero que recibe una hoja
del cielo en Vallauris,
y oye pasar los gremios a su colmena, cerca
del mar y su corona de cedro simultáneo.

Fuerte es nuestra medida cuando
arrojamos – amando al simple hombre –
tu brasa en la balanza, en la bandera.
No estaba en los designios del escorpión tu rostro.
Quiso morder a veces y encontró tu cristal
desmedido,
tu lámpara bajo la tierra
y entonces?
Entonces por la orilla de la tierra crecemos.
hacia la otra orilla de la tierra crecemos.

Quien no escuche estos pasos oye tus pasos. Oye
desde la infinidad del tiempo este camino.
Ancha es la tierra. No está tu mano sola.
Ancha es la luz. Enciéndela sobre nosotros.

the shepherd's standard: a sheep feels the caress
of a leaf tumbling from the sky at Vallauris,
hears the workers heading to their hive
by the sea, crowned with so many
simultaneous cedars.

We stand strong and tall when we arm
ordinary men and cast your embers
on to scales, on to flags.
The scorpion had no designs on your face.
Yes, it tried to bite, at times, but instead
butted against your out-sized glass
and your lamp beneath the ground.
What then?
Then we grow from one corner of the earth
to the other: we swell.
If people do not hear our footsteps, they hear yours.
They can hear you from time infinite.
The world is a wide space. Yours is not the only hand.
The light is broad. Shine it. Shine it over us.

de
LA BARCAROLA
(1967)

EL AMOR

Te amé sin por qué, sin de dónde, te amé sin mirar,
    sin medida,
y yo no sabía que oía la voz de la férrea distancia,
el eco llamando a la greda que canta por las cordilleras,
yo no suponía, chilena, que tú eras mis propias raíces,
yo sin saber cómo entre idiomas ajenos leí el alfabeto
que tus pies menudos dejaban andando en la arena
y tú sin tocarme acudías al centro del bosque invisible
a marcar el árbol de cuya corteza volaba el aroma perdido.

SONATA

Oh clara de luna, oh estatua pequeña y oscura,
oh sal, oh cuchara que saca el aroma del mundo y lo vuelca en
    mis venas,
oh cántara negra que canta a la luz del rocío,
oh piedra del río enterrado de donde colaba y volvía la noche,
oh pámpana de agua, peral de cintura fragante,
oh tesorería del bosque, oh paloma de la primavera,
oh tarjeta que deja el rocío en los dedos de la madreselva,
oh metálica noche de agosto con argollas de plata en el cielo,
oh mi amor, te pareces al tren que atraviesa el otoño en Temuco,
oh mi amada perdida en mis manos como una sortija en la
    nieve,
oh entendida en las cuerdas del viento color de guitarra
que desciende de las cordilleras, junto a Nahuilbuta llorando,
oh función matinal de la abeja buscando un secreto,

from
BOAT SONG
(1967)

LOVE

I loved without a why, without a where, I loved you without
    looking, without measure,
without realising I could hear the granite distance,
the wail of an echo answering the song of clay in the cordilleras.
I had no idea, my Chilean love, that you were my own roots,
no idea I could read the alphabet of strange tongues
that your tiny feet left paddling in the sand.
And that without touching me, you came to the core of the
    invisible forest
to carve a scar in the bark of a tree with its nomadic aroma.

SONATA

Oh moonlight, oh small, dark statue,
salt, spoon scooping the scent of the world and filling my veins
    with it,
oh amphora singing in the light of the dew
oh stone in a buried river where the night flew off and drifted back,
oh watery vine leaf, fragrant-waisted pear tree,
oh treasury abandoning the dew in honeysuckle fingers,
oh metallic August night with its silver wedding bands in the sky,
oh my love, you're like the train passing through autumn in
    Temuco,
oh my darling, lost within my grasp like a ring in the snow,
I can hear you in the strings of the guitar-coloured wind
weeping as it descends from the cordilleras near Nahuelbuta,
oh the bee on its morning rounds, sniffing out a secret,

oh edificio que el ámbar y el agua construyeron para que habitara
yo, exigente inquilino que olvida la llave y se duerme a la
    puerta,
oh corneta llevada en la grupa celestial del tritón submarino,
oh guitarra de greda sonando en la paz polvorienta de Chile,
oh cazuela de aceite y cebolla, vaporosa, olorosa, sabrosa,
oh expulsada de la geometría por arte de nube y cadera,
oh máquina de agua, oh reloja de pajarería,
oh mi amorosa, mi negra, mi blanca, mi pluma, mi escoba,
oh mi espada, mi pan y mi miel, mi canción, mi silencio,
    mi vida.

PRIMAVERA EN CHILE

Hermoso es septiembre en mi patria cubierto con una corona de
    mimbre y violetas
y con un canasto colgando en los brazos colmado de dones terrestres:
septiembre adelanta sus ojos mapuches matando el invierno
y vuelve el chileno a la resurrección de la carne y el vino.
Amable es el sábado y apenas se abrieron las manos del viernes
voló transportando ciruelas y caldos de luna y pescado.

Oh amor en la tierra que tú recorrieras que yo atravesamos
no tuve en mi boca un fulgor de sandía como Talagante
y en vano busqué entre los dedos de la geografía
el mar clamoroso, el vestido que el viento y la piedra otorgaron
    a Chile,
y no hallé duraznos de enero redondos de luz y delicia
como el terciopelo que guarda y desgrana la miel de mi patria.
Y en los matorrales del Sur sigiloso conozco el rocío
por sus penetrantes diamantes de menta, y me embriaga le
    aroma

oh house of amber and water where I
lived, a demanding tenant who forgets his keys and ends up
    sleeping in the doorway,
oh cornet carried on the rump of an underwater newt,
oh clay guitar playing in the bone-dry tranquillity of Chile,
oh casserole of oil and onions, steamy, savoury, spicy,
oh, expelled from all of geometry by clouds and hops,
oh water machine, oh clock among a flock of birds,
oh my amorous one, my black one, my white one, my feather,
    my broom.
oh my sword, my bread and honey, my song, my silence, my life.

SPRING IN CHILE

September is lovely in my country, crowned by willows and violets
and by a hanging basket brimming with earthly gifts.
Yes, September's Mapuche eyes open early to kill off winter
and the Chilean returns to the resurrection of flesh, food and wine.
Saturday is a friendly fellow and scarcely has Friday opened its
    hands
than it brings in plums and broth spiced with fish and the moon.

Oh my darling, around the world that you and I have walked,
I never tasted the radiance of Talagante watermelon.
I unclenched each of Earth's fingers, searching in vain
for Chile's clamourous sea or its dresses carved by wind and stone.
And I could never find a January peach quite as rotund with
    light and delight
as the velvet concealed and threshed by my homeland honey.
On the scrublands of the secretive South, I recognise the dew
from its penetrating diamonds of mint, and I'm intoxicated by
    the aroma

127

del vino central que estalló desde tu cinturón de racimos
y el olor de tus aguas pesqueras que te llena de olfato
porque se abren las valvas del mar en tu pecho de plata
    abundante,
y encumbrado arrastrando los pies cuando marcho en los
    montes más duros
yo diviso en la nieve invencible la razón de tu soberanía.

PUCATRIHUE

En Pucatrihue vive
la voz, la sal, el aire.

En Pucatrihue.

En Pucatrihue crece
la tarde como cuando
una bandera
nace.

En Pucatrihue.

En Pucatrihue un día
se perdió y no volvió
de la selva.

En Pucatrihue.

En Pucatrihue creo
no sé por que ni cuándo
nacieron
mis raíces.

of central Chile's wine bursting from your belt of grape
    clusters
and the scent of your fishing waters which fill our nostrils
when the valves of the sea open in your ample silver breast
and, as I drag my feet proudly over the harsh hills,
I can just make out, in the invincible snow, the reason for
    your mastery.

PUCATRIHUE

In Pucatrihue,
voices are alive,
like salt, like the air.

In Pucatrihue.

In Pucatrihue, the evening
swells like the unfurling
of a flag.

In Pucatrihue.

In Pucatrihue, a day
wandered off and never returned
from the woods.

In Pucatrihue.

In Pucatrihue,
I've no idea why or when,
it was there
that I laid down
my roots.

Las perdí por el mundo.
O las dejé olvidadas
en un hotel oscuro,
carcomido, de Europa.

Las busqué sin embargo,
y sólo hallé las minas,
los viejos esqueletos
de mármol amarillo.

Ay, Delia, mis raíces
están en Pucatrihue.
no sé por qué, ni cómo,
ni desde cuándo, pero
están en Pucatrihue.

Si.

En Pucatrihue.

SANTOS REVISITADO III

Cuando tú hacemos, cuando yo hacemos el viaje del amor,
amor, Matilde, el mar o tu boca redonda
son, somos la hora que desprendió el entonces,
y cada día corre buscando aniversario.

I strayed, travelling the world,
or left those roots behind
in some dark, shabby
hotel room in Europe.

I kept looking for them
but found nothing but mines,
ancient skeletons
of yellowing marble.

Delia, my roots
are in Pucatrihue.
I don't know why, or how,
or how long they've been there.
But they're in Pucatrihue.

Yes.

In Pucatrihue.

SANTOS REVISITED III

When you, we do, when I, we do, when we take our lovers' trip,
my love, Matilde, the sea or your round mouth
are, we are, the hour which casts off the then
and every hour races away in search of an anniversary.

LOS OFRECIMIENTOS

Desde hoy te proclamo estival, hija de oro, tristeza,
lo que quiera tu ser diminuto del ancho universo.

Bienamada, te doy o te niego, en la copa del mundo:
aun lo que explora la larva en su túnel estrecho
o lo que descifra el astrónomo en la paz parabólica
o aquella república de tristes estatuas que lloran al lado del mar
o el peso nupcial de la abeja cargada de oro oloroso
o la colección de las hojas de todo el otoño en los bosques
o un hilo del agua en la piedra que hay en mi país natalicio
o un saco de trigo arrastrado por cuatro ladrones hambrientos
o un trono de mimbre tejido por las elegantes arañas de Angol
o un par de zapatos cortados en piedra de luna
o un huevo nacido de cóndor de las cordilleras de Chile
o siete semillas de hierba fragante crecida a la orilla del
        río Ralún
o la flor especial que se abre en las nubes a causa del humo
o el rito de los araucanos con un caballito de palo en la selva
o aquel tren que perdi en California y encontré en el desierto
        de Gobi
o el ala del ave relámpago en cuya ancestral cacería
anduve perdido en el Sur y olvidado por todo un invierno
o el lápiz marino capaz de escribir en las olas
y lo que tú quieras y lo que no quieras te doy y te niego
porque las palabras estallan abriendo el castillo, y cerramos
        los ojos.

OFFERINGS

From today onwards, I name you summer, daughter of gold,
    sadness,
anything you want, tiny creature in this vast universe.

My darling, I give you or deny you all of this on the crest of the world:
the burrowing of the larva in its narrow tunnel,
the astronomer's discoveries in his parabolic peace,
or that republic of statues weeping by the sea
or the nuptial weight of the bee with its sweet scent of gold
or the leaves collected in the woods throughout autumn
or a trickle of water over a stone in my homeland
or a sack of wheat dragged by four starving thieves
or a wicker throne woven by elegant spiders in Angol
or a pair of shoes carved from moonstone
or an egg laid by a condor from the cordilleras of Chile
or seven seeds of fragrant grass growing on the banks of the
    River Ralún
or the special flower blooming in the clouds thanks to the smoke
or the Araucanian ritual of a rocking horse in the forest
or the train I missed in California and caught in the Gobi Desert
or the wings of the fleet-footed bird I hunted with my ancestors
in the South, lost and forgotten a whole winter long,
or the sea pencil capable of writing in the waves
anything you want and do not want, I give you and deny you
because when words explode, breaching the castle, we
    close our eyes.

de
LA ESPADA ENCENDIDA
(1970)

ARGUMENTO

En esta fábula se relata la historia de un fugitivo de las grandes devastaciones que terminaron con la humanidad. Fundador de un reino emplazado en las espaciosas soledades magallánicas, se decide a ser el último habitante del mundo, hasta que aparece en su territorio una doncella evadida de la ciudad áurea de los Césares.

El destino que los llevó a confundirese levanta contra ellos la antigua espada encendida del nuevo Edén salvaje y solitario.

Al producirse la cólera y la muerte de Dios, en la escena iluminada por el gran volcán, estos seres adánicos toman conciencia de su propia divinidad.

IX EL HALLAZGO

El fundador detuvo el paso: Rosía Verde
parecía un pedazo desprendido a la luna:
un cuerpo horizontal caído de la noche:
un silencio desnudo entre las hojas.

Amó de nuevo Rhodo con tormento,
con furia sigilosa, con dolor:
cada sombra en sus ojos le parecía un desdén,
y la inmovilidad de su novia campestre
hizo dudar a Rhodo de la dicha:
a quién reservó la suave su suavidad de musgo?
para quién destinó sus anteriores manos?

from
THE FLAMING SWORD
(1970)

THE STORY

This fable tells the story of a fugitive from the great dev-
astation which ended humanity. The founder of a kingdom
in the Magellanic solitude, he sets out to become the last inhabitant on earth until he comes across a girl who has fled
from the golden City of the Caesars.

Fate, which drove them into each other's arms, conspires
to wield the ancient flaming sword against then in this new
Eden, so wild and desolate.

As God dies in a fit of rage – a scene illuminated by the
great volcano – the 'Adam and Eve' lovers become aware of
their own divinity.

IX THE DISCOVERY

The founder paused: Rosía Verde
looked like a piece of the moon
fallen to earth from the night sky,
silent and naked among the leaves.

Rhodo loved her again with stealth,
fury, torment and agony;
he was speared by the scorn
in the shadow of her eyes
and as she lay there,
his rustic lover, without moving,
he feared for his happiness.
For whom was she keeping her gentle moss
and were her hands remembering the past?

135

en qué estaba pensando con los ojos cerrados?
Pedía posesión de su cuerpo y su miel,
de su cada minuto y cada pelo,
posesión de su sueño y de sus párpados,
de su sexo hasta el fondo, de sus pies labradores,
de su pasado entero, de su día siguiente,
de sus sutiles huellas en la nieve
y mientras más la tuvo, devorándola
en el abrazo cuerpo a cuerpo que los aniquilaba,
él parecía consumirla menos,
como si la galana de los bosques, la huérfana,
la muchacha casual con aroma de leña
hubiera abierto una herida como un pozo sus pies
y por allí cayera el trueno que él trajo al mundo.
Rhodo reconoció su derrota besando
en la boca de Rosía su propio amor salvaje
y ella se estremeció como si la quemara
un rayo de oro que encendió su sexo
y paseó el incendio sobre su alma.

X LAS FIERAS

Se deseaban, se lograban, se destruían,
se ardían, se rompían, se caían de bruces
el uno dentro del otro, en una lucha a muerte,
se enmarañaban, se perseguían, se odiaban,
se buscaban, se destrozaban de amor,
volvían a temerse y a maldecirse y a amarse,
se negaban cerrando los ojos. Y los puños
de Rosía golpeaban el muro de noche,
sin dormir, mientras Rhodo desde su almena cruel

Who was she thinking of, with her eyes closed fast?
He asked permission to possess her body,
her honey, every hair and every minute,
her dreams and her eyelids,
the depths of her sex, her working girl's feet,
the whole of her past, the days to come,
her subtle footsteps in the snow.
And the more he possessed her,
the more he devoured her body
in an embrace that annihilated them both,
the less she was consumed,
as if this beautiful orphan of the forest,
perfumed by firewood,
had appeared by chance
and opened a wound as deep as a well,
a chasm to catch Rhodo's thunder.
Rhodo recognised his defeat, kissed her,
left his savage love on Rosía's lips.
She trembled, as if her sex were inflamed
by gilded lightning, and her soul was ablaze.

X THE SAVAGES

They desired each other, won each other,
destroyed each other, burned each other,
fell headlong inside one another
in a battle to the last, tangled with each other,
chased each other, hated one another,
sought each other armed with deadly passion,
feared each other, cursed each other, loved one another
and closed their eyes to deny each other.
Rosía's fists pummelled the night.
Neither could sleep: Rhodo, from his cruel rampart,

vigilaba el peligro de las fieras despiertas
sabiendo que él llevaba el puma en su sangre,
y aullaba un león agónico en la noche sin sueño
de Rhodo, y la mañana le traía
a su novia desnuda, cubierta de rocío,
fresca de nieve como una paloma,
incierta aún entre el amor y el odio,
y allí los dos inciertos resplandecían de nuevo
mordiéndose y besándose y arrastrándose el lecho
en donde se quedaba desmayada la furia.

XII EL CONOCIMIENTO

Varona, dijo el señor silvestre,
por qué sabemos que estamos desnudos?
Todos los frutos nos pertenecían
y los siete volcanes iracundos supieron
que sin tus ojos yo no podía vivir,
que sin tu cuerpo entraba en la agonía
y sin tu ser me sentía perdido.

Ahora la ciudadela sin murallas,
las cascadas de sal, la luna en los cipreses,
la selva de rabiosas raíces, el silencio,
los muermos estrellados, la soledad vacía,
acuática, volcánica, la que busqué a pesar
y en contra de mí mismo, el reino amargo,
tempestuoso, fundado a sol y a lluvia,
con las estatuas muertas del pasado
y el rumor de la primavera en las abejas del ulmo,
la espesura que el canto del chucao taladra

protected them from the rousing beasts,
feeling kinship with the puma in his blood.
A dying lion's howls pierced the night
and in the morning, Rosía lay naked,
dew-coated, cool as snow like a dove,
still unsure between hate and love.
They doubted once more and then,
the fever took hold again
and drove them biting and kissing
to the bed where all fury fainted away.

XII AWARENESS

Dear girl, the savage man says,
how do we know we're naked?
Every fruit is ours to eat
and the seven volcanoes,
in their wrath, know this:
that I cannot live without your eyes,
that I'd be lost without you.
that I would die without your body beside me.

And now the citadel with no walls,
the moon in the cypresses, the salty waterfalls,
the jungle with its raging roots,
the silence, the star-lit tedium and solitude:
empty, aquatic, volcanic loneliness –
I sought it out despite myself:
the harsh domain, tempestuous,
built on sun and rain, the corpses
of statues and spring's retorts,
the bees in the ulmo trees,
the birdsong of the chucao

como risa o sollozo o exhalación o fuga
y los nevados, de Ralún, donde comienza
el terrible archipiélago con sus campanas de frío,
Varona mia, Evarosa, Rosaflor,
se despiden de mi, porque sabemos.

Es la selva del árbol de la vida. El racimo
de cada planta, el peso de la fruta salvaje,
nos nutrió de repente, y estuvimos desnudos
hasta morir de amor y de dolor.

XL LA FLOR AZUL

Rhodo cortó una flor y la dejó en su lecho.
Era una flor de linaje violeta,
semiazul, entreabierta como un ojo
de la profundidad del mar distante.

Dejo Rhodo esa flor bajo Rosía
y ella durmió sobre la flor azul.

Toda esa noche soñó con el mar.

Una ola redonda se la llevó en el sueño
hasta una roca de color azul.

trilling and drilling like laughter
or like sobs or the escape of a sigh,
and the snow-capped mountains
in Ralún, where the icy bells
of the dread archipelago begin to toll.
We know all this, my love, we know:
which is why Evarosa and Rosaflor
are abandoned in the snow.

This is the forest with its tree of life.
We fed off the flesh of every plant,
the body of every wild fruit,
and we were naked, dying again
from love and pain.

XL THE BLUE FLOWER

Rhodo cut a flower and left it
in her bed. It was a violet,
a blue, half-open eye,
carried from the depths of a distant sea.

Rhodo placed the flower beneath Rosía
and she slept on it and dreamed.

Dreamed of the sea all night.

Dreamed that the curve of a wave
swept her on to a rock. Blue. And there

Allí esperaba ella por años y por siglos
entre la espuma repetida y el
cabeceo de los cachalotes.
                         Sola
está Rosía hasta que luego
el cielo descendió de su estatura
y la cubrió con una nube azul.

Al despertar del sueño bajo sus ancas claras
y entre sus piernas una flor caliente:
todo su cuerpo era una luz azul.

Rosía waited for years, centuries,
alone with the head-tossing whales
in the gathering foam.
Till the sky fell and covered her
in blankets of cloud. Blue.

Waking up, she discovered the flower,
hot between her fair thighs:
her whole body shimmered. Blue.

Geografía infructuosa
(1972)

FELICIDAD

Sin duda, sí, contesto
sin que nadie pregunte y me pregunte:
lo bueno es ya sin interrogaciones,
sin compromiso, responder
a nuestra sombra lenta y sucesiva.

Sí, en este tiempo mío, en esta historia
de puerta personal, acumulé
no el desvarío sino la nostalgia
y la enterré en la casa de cemento:
duelo o dolor de ayer no me acompañan
porque no sólo se mueren los huesos,
la piel, los ojos, la palabra, el humo,
sino también el llanto devorado
por las sesenta bocas de la vida.

Así de lo que de uno en otro sitio
guardé – tristeza o súbita amargura –
la devolví cual pesca temblorosa
al mar, al mar, y me acosté desnudo.

Ésta es la explicación de mi ventura:
yo tengo el sueño duro de la piedra.

from
FRUITLESS GEOGRAPHY
(1972)

HAPPINESS

I can answer without hesitation,
before anyone asks me or I even
ask myself: it's so good to be free
of interrogations, commitments,
to respond to the slow spread of our shadow.

Yes, at my time of life, in my own story,
at my own gateway, I accumulated
nostalgia, not delirium,
and I buried it in a cement house.
Yesterday's pain and grief are no longer with me
because it's not just bones
and skin and eyes and words and smoke that die
but the tears devoured by
life's sixty hungry mouths.

So all that sadness or sudden bitterness
I'd stored up, I simply tossed back in the sea,
as if it were writhing in my hands like a fish,
and went to bed naked.

That's the secret of my happiness:
I sleep as heavily as a stone.

EL COBARDE

Y ahora, a dolerme el alma y todo el cuerpo,
a gritar, a escondernos en el pozo
de la infancia, con miedo y ventarrón:
hoy nos trajo el sol joven del invierno
una gota de sangre, un signo amargo
y ya se acabó todo: no hay remedio,
no hay mundo, ni bandera prometida;
basta una herida para derribarte:
con una sola letra
te mata el alfabeto de la muerte,
un solo pétalo del gran dolor humano
cae en tu orina y crees
que el mundo se desangra.

Así, con sol frío de Francia, en mes de marzo,
a fines del invierno dibujado
por negros árboles de la Normandía
con el cielo entreabierto ya al destello
de dulces días, flores venideras,
yo encogido, sin calles ni vitrinas,
callada mi campana de cristal,
con mi pequeña espina lastimosa
voy sin vivir, ya mineralizado,
inmóvil esperando la agonía,
mientras florece el territorio azul
predestinado de la primavera.

Mi verdad o mi fábula revelan
que es más tenaz que el hombre
el ejercicio de la cobardía.

THE COWARD

And now, time for my soul and my whole body to hurt,
to cry out, to hide away in the shaft
of my youth, in fear, tossed around by gusts.
Today, the young, wintry sun
brought us a drop of blood, a bitter sign,
and it's all over: there's no way out,
no promised land or flag:
a single wound's enough to bring you down;
a single letter from the alphabet of death,
a single petal from the vast human hurt
falls into your urine and it seems as though
the whole world's bleeding dry.

And so, in a cold French sun in March,
at the end of a winter sketched out
among the black trees of Normandy,
under a sky half-open to the glimmer
of sweeter days, the flowers to come,
I'm shy and shrunken, hiding from
streets and shop windows.
Even my glass bell is silenced.
I drag my pitiful backbone
and wander, lifeless as mineral,
motionless, awaiting the end
while the land turns blue
in the predestined blossoming of spring.

Truth, or fable, proves that cowardice
is a stubborn act, more stubborn
than man himself.

de
INCITACIÓN AL NIXONICIDIO
(1973)]

AQUÍ ME QUEDO

Yo no quiero la Patria dividida

ni por siete cuchillos desangrada:
quiero la luz de Chile enarbolada
sobre la nueva casa construida:

cabemos todos en la tierra mía.

Y que los que se creen prisioneros
se vayan lejos con su melodía:

siempre los ricos fueron extranjeros.
Que se vayan a Miami con sus tías!

Yo me quedo a cantar con los obreros
en esta nueva historia y geografía

from
INCITEMENT TO NIXONICIDE
(1973)

I'M HERE TO STAY

I do not want my homeland divided

or bled dry by seven knives.
I want the light of Chile raised
over this newly built home of ours:

there's room for us all in this land of mine.

And those who think they're prisoners
can take their melodies far, far away.

The rich were always foreign –
let them join their aunts in Miami.

I'm staying to sing with the workers
to our new history and geography.

XIV

Evtuchenko es un loco,
es un *clown*,
así dicen con boca cerrada.
Ven, Evtuchenko,
vamos a no conversar,
ya lo hemos hablado todo
antes de llegar a este mundo,
y hay en tu poesía
rayos de luna nueva,
pétalos electrónicos,
locomotoras,
lágrimas,
y de cuando en cuando, hola!
arriba! abajo!
tus piruetas, tus altas acrobacias.
Y por qué no un payaso?

Nos faltan en el mundo
Napoleón, un *clown* de las batallas
(perdido más tarde en la nieve),
Picasso, *clown* del cosmos,
bailando en el altar
de los milagros,
Y Colón, aquel payaso triste
que humillado en todas las pistas
nos descubrió hace siglos.
Sólo al poeta no quieren dejarlo,
quieren robarle su pirueta,
quieren quitarle su salto mortal.

from
ELEGY
(1974)

XIV

Yevtushenko is a madman,
He's a clown,
that's what they're saying through gritted teeth.
Come here, Yevtushenko,
let's sit down and talk about nothing at all.
We've already discussed it all
before we were even born
And your poetry
grips the light of the New Moon.
Electronic petals,
locomotives,
tears,
and from time to time, a 'hello;,
an 'up above', a 'below,
all your pirouettes, your high-wire acrobatics.
And why not: a clown?

The world needs a Napoleon,
a battleground clown
(who ends up lost in the snow),
Picasso, the clown of the cosmos,
dancing on the altar
of miracles,
and Columbus, that sad clown
humiliated everywhere he went
but who discovered us
so many centuries ago.
It's only the poet they won't leave alone.
They want to steal his pirouettes,
remove his right to take a fatal jump.

Yo lo defiendo
contra los nuevos filisteos.
Adelante Evtuchenko,
mostremos en el circo
nuestra destreza y nuestra tristeza,
nuestro placer de jugar con la luz
para que la verdad relampaguee
entre sombra y sombra.
Hurrah!
ahora entremos,
que se apague la sala y con un reflector
alúmbrennos las caras
para que así puedan ver
dos alegres pájaros
dispuestos a llorar con todo el mundo.

I defend him
Against all the new Philistines,
Come on, Yevtushenko,
let's head for the circus
and show off our skills and our ills,
the joy we put into playing with the light
so that the truth will beam out
once again
from among the shadows.
Hurray!
Let's step on stage together.
tell them to dim the auditorium
and turn the spotlight on our faces:
They'll see two happy birds
preparing to weep with the rest of the world.

de
DEFECTOS ESCOGIDOS
(1974)

EL INCOMPETENTE

Nací tan malo para competir
que Pedro y Juan se lo llevaban todo:
las pelotas,
las chicas,
las aspirinas y los cigarrillos.

Es difícil la infancia para un tonto
y como yo fui
siempre más tonto que los otros tontos
me birlaron los lápices, las gomas
y los primeros besos de Temuco.

Ay, aquellas muchachas!
Nunca vi unas princesas como ellas,
eran todas azules o enlutadas,
claras como cebollas, como el nácar,
manos de precisión, narices puras,
ojos insoportables de caballo,
pies como peces o como azucenas.

Lo cierto es que yo anduve
esmirriado y cubriendo con orgullo
mi condición de enamorado idiota,
sin atreverme a mirar una pierna
ni aquel pelo detrás de la cabeza
que caía como una catarata
de aguas oscuras sobre mis deseos.

Después, señores, me pasó lo mismo
por todos los caminos donde anduve,
de un codazo o con dos ojos fríos
me eliminaban de la competencia,

THE INCOMPETENT ONE

I was born so bad at competing
that any Dick and Harry won the prizes:
every game,
every girl,
even the aspirin and the cigarettes.

Childhood is difficult for a fool,
and since I was always
stupider than the other fools,
they stole my pencils, my rubbers
and the first kisses in Temuco.

Oh, those girls!
I never saw such princesses,
all in blue or mourning,
bright as onions or mother of pearl,
with their precise, pure hands and noses,
their gaze as fixed as a horse's
and their like fish or lilies.

It's true: I was a scrawny youth,
proudly concealing my condition.
I was a love-struck idiot,
too frightened to stare at a girl's leg
or the hair tumbling
like a waterfall behind her:
that was dark water on my desires.

And ladies and gentlemen, the same thing
kept on happening, wherever I went.
They ejected me from the competition
with an elbow or two cold eyes.

no me dejaban ir al comedor,
todos se iban de largo con sus rubias.

Y yo no sirvo para rebelarme.

Esto de andar luciendo
méritos o medallas escondidas,
nobles acciones, títulos secretos,
no va con mi pasmada idiosincrasia;
yo me hundo en mi agujero
y de cada empujón que me propinan
retrocediendo en la zoología
me fui como los topos, tierra abajo,
buscando un subterráneo confortable
donde no me visiten ni las moscas.

Esa es mí triste historia
aunque posiblemente menos triste
que la suya, señor,
ya que también posiblemente pienso,
pienso que usted es aun más tonto todavía.

PARODIA DEL GUERRERO

Y qué hacen allá abajo?
Parecen que andan todos ocupados,
hirviendo en sus negocios.

Allá abajo, allá abajo
allá lejos,
andan tal vez estrepitosamente
de aquí no se ve mucho,

They barred me from dining rooms
and left with a blonde on each arm.

I am a useless rebel.

I'm not one for showing off
my merits or the medals lying in a drawer,
the noble acts and the secret honours.
I'm too bewildered for any of that:
I bury myself in a hole,
scuttling away from every blow,
retreating with the other animals,
like a mole, burrowing deep
in search of comforts below ground,
where even the flies can't visit me.

So there's my sad story.
And yet, it's probably a little less sad
than yours, ladies and gentlemen.
Because I get the impression
that you're even more idiotic than I am.

THE WARRIOR'S PARODY

And what are you doing down there?
You all seem to be pretty busy,
stewing over your business deals.

Down there, down there,
way down there,
you're probably making quite a racket.
I can't see much from here,

no les veo las bocas,
no les veo
detalles, sonrisas
o zapatos derrotados.
Pero, por qué no vienen?
Dónde van a meterse?

Aquí estoy, aquí estoy,
soy el campeón mental de ski, de box,
de carrera pesada,
de alas negras,
soy el verdugo,
soy el sacerdote,
soy el más general de las batallas,
no me dejen,
no, por ningún motivo,
no se vayan,
aquí tengo un reloj,
tengo una bala,
tengo un proyecto de guerrilla bancaria,
soy capaz de todo,
soy padre de todos ustedes,
hijos malditos:
qué pasa,
me olvidaron?

Desde aquí arriba los veo:
qué torpes son sin mis pies,
sin mis consejos,
qué mal se mueven en el pavimento,
no saben nada del sol,
no conocen la pólvora,
tienen que aprender a ser niños,
a comer, a invadir,
a subir las montañas,
a organizar los cuadernos,

can't see your mouths,
can't make out the details, the smiles
or the tattered shoes.
But why are you not coming up?
Where exactly are you headed?

Here I am, here I am.
In my mind, I'm a champion skier, boxer,
a black-winged, heavyweight runner.
I'm the executioner,
I'm the priest,
I'm the broadest of battles.
Don't leave me,
No, don't go,
not for any reason.
I have a watch on me.
I have a bullet,
I'm planning to start up a bankers' guerrilla movement.
I'm capable of anything, actually.
I'm the father of you all,
wretched children.
What's the matter,
have you forgotten who I am?

I can see you from up here:
how clumsy you look without my feet,
without my advice,
You're tottering along the road,
you haven't seen the sun,
you don't know what gunpowder looks like, either.
You've got to learn to be children,
to eat, to invade,
to climb mountains,
or keep your exercise books in order,

a matarse las pulgas,
a descifrar el territorio,
a descubrir las islas.

Ha terminado todo.

Se han ido por sus calles a sus guerras,
a sus indiferencias, a sus camas.
Yo me quedé pegado
entre los dientes de la soledad
como un pedazo de carne mascada
como el hueso anterior
de una bestia extinguida.

No hay derecho! Reclamo
mi dirección zonal, mis oficinas,
el rango que alcancé en el regimiento,
en la cancha de los peloteros,
y no me resigno a la sombra.

Tengo sed, apetito de luz,
y sólo trago sombra.

EL GRAN ORINADOR

El gran orinador era amarillo
y el chorro que cayó
era una lluvia color de bronce
sobre las cúpulas de las iglesias,
sobre los techos de los automóviles,
sobre las fábricas y los cementerios,
sobre la multitud y sus jardines.

to kill fleas,
to map out the territory
and discover new islands.

It's all over,

You've gone off to your wars,
to your indifference, to your beds.
And here I am, wedged
in the teeth of solitude
like a piece of chewed meat,
like the old bone
of an extinct beast.

It's not fair! I demand
my address back, my offices,
the rank I reached in the regiment,
on the football pitch.
I refuse to stay in the dark.

I'm thirsty, hungry for the light,
and yet I'm swallowing nothing but shadows.

THE GREAT URINATOR

The great urinator was yellow
and his piss was
bronze-coloured rain
falling on church domes,
on car roofs,
on factories and cemeteries,
on crowds and gardens.

Quién era, dónde estaba?

Era una densidad, líquido espeso
lo que caía
como desde un caballo
y asustados transeúntes
sin paraguas
buscaban hacia el cielo,
mientras las avenidas se anegaban
y por debajo de las puertas
entraban los orines incansables
que iban llenando acequias, corrompiendo
pisos de mármol, alfombras,
escaleras.

Nada se divisaba. Dónde
estaba el peligro?

Qué iba a pasar en el mundo?

El gran orinador desde su altura
callaba y orinaba.

Qué quiere decir esto?

Soy un simple poeta,
no tengo empeño en descifrar enigmas,
ni en proponer paraguas especiales.

Hasta luego! Saludo y me retiro
a un país donde no me hagan preguntas.

Who was he? Where was he?

His was a thick, viscous liquid
toppling, as if
from a horse.
Startled passers-by
(those without umbrellas)
squinted up at the sky
while the urine drenched the streets,
seeped tirelessly
beneath doors, filling gutters,
gnawing away at floorboards,
carpets, stairways.

But no one noticed.
Where was the danger?

What the hell would happen to the world?
The great urinator up on high
kept on pissing in total silence.

What does all this mean?

I'm a simple poet.
It's not my job to solve riddles
or design special umbrellas.

So, hello and goodbye: I'm off
to a place where no one asks me questions.

PABLO NERUDA, 'the greatest poet of the twentieth century in any language' (in the words of Gabriel García Márquez), was born in Parral, central Chile, in 1904. His second collection of poems, *Twenty Love Poems of Despair and a Song of Despair*, first published in 1924, has become the world's best-selling book of poetry in the Spanish language. He served as Chilean consul in the Far East in the 1920s, Argentina and Spain in the 1930s, and Ambassador to France in the early 1970s. His experiences during the Spanish Civil War, and in particular the murder of his great friend, the Spanish poet, Federico García Lorca, in August 1936, brought about a major metamorphosis in his poetry: it became a weapon for social and political justice. In Neruda's remarkable life, actions could be as significant as words. He saved the lives of more than 2,000 Spanish Republican refugees from Franco's fascism, shipping them out from southern France to Valparaíso, in Chile, aboard a fishing-boat, the *Winnipeg*, in 1939. And in 1948, he was forced into hiding for a year after denouncing the dictatorial Chilean regime of President Gabriel González Videla. During that year, he wrote much of his potent epic of personal and historic betrayal, *Canto General*, before escaping across the Andes on horseback. Among the riches of Neruda's many other collections, the magnificent first two volumes of *Residence on Earth* contain poems of hermetic beauty and formidable lyrical intensity. The *Elementary Odes* are elegant, sensual and life-affirming songs to everyday objects. The profoundly moving love poems in *The Captain's Verses*, the marvellously witty self-mockery of *Extravagaria* and the poignant seven books of posthumous verse are all to be relished, as are his exhilarating *Memoirs*.

Neruda was awarded the Nobel Prize for Literature in 1971. He died in Santiago on September 23, 1973, just twelve days after Augusto Pinochet's military coup. In April 2013, his body was exhumed to investigate the possibility that he might have been poisoned by his political enemies in hospital. The forensic tests continue to this day. Meanwhile, 46 years after his death, Neruda's lyrical love poetry, humanism and, above all, his infectious passion for life remain as vital and relevant as they ever were.

ADAM FEINSTEIN is an acclaimed British author, poet, translator, Hispanist, journalist, film critic and autism researcher. His biography of the Nobel Prize-winning poet, *Pablo Neruda: A Passion for Life*, was first published by Bloomsbury in 2004 and reissued in an updated edition in 2013 (Harold Pinter called it 'a masterpiece'). His book of translations from Neruda's *Canto General*, with colour illustrations by the celebrated Brazilian artist, Ana Maria Pacheco, was published by Pratt Contemporary in 2013. He also wrote the introduction to the Folio Edition of Jorge Luis Borges' *Labyrinths*, which appeared in 2007. He is currently working on a novel and a book of translations from the great Nicaraguan poet, Rubén Darío.

Feinstein has published numerous articles and book chapters, including: 'Friends or foes? The troubled personal and literary relationship between Pablo Neruda and César Vallejo' in *Politics, Poetics, Affect: Re-visioning César Vallejo* (Cambridge Scholars Publishing, 2013), and 'Pablo Neruda' in the *Cambridge Companion to Latin American Literature* (Cambridge University Press, 2018).

His own poems and his translations (of Neruda, Federico García Lorca, Mario Benedetti and others) have appeared in numerous magazines, including *PN Review, Agenda, Acumen, Poem* and *Modern Poetry in Translation*. His books on autism, *A History of Autism: Conversations with the Pioneers* (Wiley-Blackwell, 2010) and *Autism Works: A Guide to Successful Employment Across the Entire Spectrum* (Routledge, 2018), were also widely praised.

He has given numerous lectures on Neruda and autism around the world, including Chile, Mexico, Argentina, Nicaragua, the United States, Russia, China, India, Spain, Italy, Germany, Switzerland and the Netherlands. His presentations in the UK include talks at Cambridge and Oxford Universities and at the Royal Society in London. He broadcasts regularly for the BBC and writes for the *Guardian*, the *Observer*, the *Financial Times* and the *Times Literary Supplement*. He is a Royal Literary Fund Fellow.

165

W . P . Gammon .